This book is a
Gift

from

_____

to

_____

on the occasion of

_____

date

_____

100 Reasons Why Sex Must Wait Until Marriage

DR. D. K. OLUKOYA

100 Reasons Why Sex Must Wait Until Marriage

(c) 2012 DR. D. K. OLUKOYA

ISBN: 978-978-920-017-7

A publication of

Mountain of Fire and Miracles Ministries
International Headquarters, Lagos Nigeria.

All scripture quotations are from the King James Version of the Bible. Unless otherwise stated.

Cover page illustration by Pastor (Mrs.) Shade Olukoya

Acknowledgements

*I would like to appreciate the
effort of my dear wife,
Pastor (Mrs.)
Shade Olukoya,
and her support and positive
contributions. She has been a
pillar, and worked behind the
scenes for the success of the
ministry. Thanks for being there
all the time,
I Love You!*

●●●

Preface

*I*f I claim to be your friend, then I must tell you this truth. The Mountain of Fire and Miracles Ministries is not a cosmetic church and I am not a cosmetician. I am a surgeon and the job of a surgeon is to look at what is not good and then cut it out, no matter how hard it is. In the past, to relieve injury from glass fragment piercing one's foot, a very hot knife doused in palm oil is applied on the injury. Of course, it is a very painful process which may make the sufferer scream and cry, but at the end of the day, the injury is healed. That is what happens in life sometimes as well. What helps you may be very painful but it heals you at the end.

I have been born again for years and I have been in the ministerial work for years. One area the enemy has used to paralyze, not only marital lives but also destinies, is the area I have explored in this book.

Sex is a mystery, and unfortunately majority of those who engage in it do not fully understand the mystery behind it. The only thing most people understand about it is the pleasure derived from it and the procreation that can result from it. Many do not understand that when sex is not done within the scripturally prescribed confines of marriage, the temporary pleasure derived can lead to eternal pressure.

There are a lot of people today at the Prayer City and almost all branches of MFM all over the world that are undergoing the deliverance which they would not have needed, if they had waited for marriage before having sex. The reason why a lot of stubborn problems in many lives have refused to yield ground to aggressive prayers is because such lives have been sexually defiled. As a result, instead of their prayers to attract mercy from heaven, it attracts anger. That is why I have taken time to unlock some of the mysteries of sex in this book. Considerable attention has also been given to the after-effects of premarital sex which go to show why you should wait until marriage before engaging in it. Some of these consequences are medical, so I have drawn from my training as a microbiologist to explain a good number of sexually transmitted diseases (STDs) and their symptoms. Steps are also listed on how you can stay pure and avoid sex until marriage. Sex outside marriage is a killer and it has successfully destroyed millions of destinies. Do not let yours be next! It is the focus of this book, therefore, to show the need to wait until marriage before having sex.

The Lord Jesus Christ shall give you the grace to abide by His words, in the name of Jesus.

Your friend,

Dr. Daniel Olukoya

TABLE *of* CONTENTS

Chapter

One

SEX,
What A Mystery!

The fact is that sex was designed by God. Just
like every other thing He created, it was very
good and is still very good as long as you follow
His commandments on it.

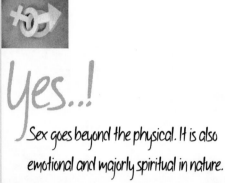

Yes..!

Sex goes beyond the physical. It is also
emotional and majorly spiritual in nature.

There is still a lot of ignorance about the spiritual
aspect of sex...further compounded because the
world today, in the name of modernity and
civilization, has changed its values on sex.

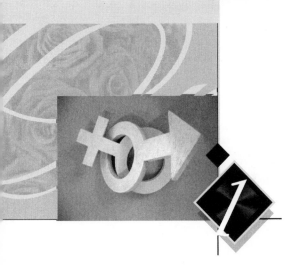

SEX, WHAT A MYSTERY!

*O*NE OF THE MYSTERIES which humanity as a whole is very ignorant of today is sex. While a lot of research has been done on the physiology of sex, that is, sexual organs and hormones among others, there is still a lot of ignorance about the spiritual aspect of sex. Yes, sex goes beyond the physical. It is also emotional and majorly spiritual in nature. This ignorance has been further compounded because the world today, in the name of modernity and civilization, has changed its values on sex. The Word of God is no longer the standard upon which sexual values are defined. This is one of the signs of the end times and it has been predicted in the Bible.

2 Timothy 4:3-4

> *"For the time will come when they will not endure sound doctrine; but after their own lusts shall they heap to themselves teachers, having itching ears; And they shall turn away their ears from the truth, and shall be turned unto fables."*

It is sad to say that some church denominations have joined the compromise on some of these values and teach all forms of heresy with regards to sex. However, Jesus will never change and cannot be modernized; he remains the same.

Hebrews 13:8

> *"Jesus Christ the same yesterday, and today, and forever."*

The fact is that sex was designed by God. Just like every other thing He created, it was very good and is still very good as long as you follow His commandments on it. Man had no problem with God until He disobeyed the command not to eat of the tree of the knowledge of good and evil. The same thing applies to sex. Unfortunately, a lot of people think that sex was the fruit which God asked man not to eat. This has led to sex being referred to as the 'forbidden fruit' in popular culture. This is however not true.

APPLYING THE RIGHT THERAPY

It is not everything that yields to prayer. Some things don't yield to prayer; they yield to repentance. Some people also think everything is all about deliverance. Certain things do not require deliverance; they only submit to character re-arrangement. The same thing goes for fasting. Some problems cannot be solved by fasting; they can only be resolved by application of the Word of God. Faith is also not a panacea. There are times· you need to pray enquiry prayers to know why you are in a situation and not just using blind faith, believing that you have got out, whereas you are free, whereas you are still in the enemy's cage.

1 Corinthians 6:18-20

> *"Flee fornication. Every sin that a man doeth is without the body; but he that committeth fornication sinneth against his own body. What? Know ye not that your body is the temple of the Holy Ghost which is in you, which ye have of God, and ye are not your own? For ye are bought with a price: therefore glorify God in your body, and in your spirit, which are God's."*

For other sins in the Bible; the formula given is to resist them. For example, it says, *"Resist the devil and he will flee from you."* But in this case, the Bible makes it clear that you should not even bother to resist or confront it; simply flee! If that confuses you, it means run as fast as your feet can carry you and as far away as you can go. If Samson had fled from Delilah, we will not be reading a bad history about him today. I pray for you that you will not have a bad history, in the name of Jesus. Another lesson we can derive from this verse is that every other sin is outside your own body. But fornication is a sin against your own body.

> *It is not everything that yields to prayer. Some things don't yield to prayer; they yield to repentance... Certain things do not require deliverance; they only submit to character re-arrangement. The same thing goes for fasting.*

Right from the beginning of Scripture to this time, God has never worked with majority. But minority with God is a winner. Majority without God is a loser. The whole world was destroyed in the days of Noah and only a few people: eight souls entered the ark. A lot of people left Egypt to go to the Promised Land but only two out of three million got there. Jesus had five hundred disciples, but in the Upper Room, only one hundred and twenty were found there. So all through history, we find that God has always dealt with minority and the fact that the majority are doing a thing does not mean that thing is right. The largeness of the number of people traveling on the wrong road does not make it the right road.

A large number of people who are still single today could have been happily married now if they practiced sex after marriage. A lot of people do not realize that there are some covenants attached to them that prevent marriage after pre-marital sex. If they had kept themselves and not engaged in sexual intercourse, their relationship would have resulted in marriage. But the moment they allowed their partner to sleep with them, the prospect of marriage vanished into thin air.

When you release yourself sexually to somebody, it blocks your vision, removes you from the power of the Almighty and brings a lot of deep bondage to your life. I am telling you the truth from my heart. If I do not tell you this, I will be subjecting myself to God's judgment and it shall also be a waste of your time. There are some things that require peculiar methods which we must sit down and look at thoroughly.

I must have prayed for over ten thousand ladies that pushed themselves into such bondages that result from unlawful sexual act. They just allowed someone to sleep with them and as a result, lost their marriage. The enemy who knows your future and your destiny will always organize somebody to sleep with you outside marriage, in order to gain a foothold in your life. Once he successfully does that, he pushes you into the arena where there will be no connection with the Most High. And then to get answers to prayers for marriage becomes very hard, if not impossible.

God has never worked with majority. But minority with God is a winner. Majority without God is a loser. The whole world was destroyed in the days of Noah and only a few people: eight souls entered the ark.

SEX IS MORE THAN A PHYSICAL UNION OF THE SEXUAL ORGANS OF THE BODY

Sex is actually very potent and the power contained in it can be compared with atomic energy. Atomic energy is very useful and contains immense power, but when used towards a negative end, it becomes a destructive weapon. The same atomic energy that can generate enough electricity to power a city can also destroy a city when it is used as a bomb. The terrible thing about it is that it eliminates and wipes out lives completely. The same thing also applies to sex. Sex is a powerful force created by God for many beneficial reasons. But at the same time it can destroy, if not used properly. As pointed out earlier, sex is not only a physical thing; it is also a spiritual thing. Immediately you complete the act of sexual intercourse with someone, you have a bonding with the person: whether you know him or her or not, like him or her or not: it does not really matter. There is a bond already in existence and it can cause the transfer and exchange of both curses and blessings. So as a young lady, if you are still a virgin and someone you are not married to is saying 'I want to sleep with you'; what he/she is really saying is that 'I want to destroy your life'. It brings curses. It can bring barriers, death, and prevent marriage.

There was a boy who lived in Victoria Island, an affluent community in Lagos, a cosmopolitan city and the commercial hub of Nigeria. The parents just noticed that he was always unwilling to let anyone see his nakedness, either male or female. While in the bathroom he locked the door securely and while in bed he wore his pyjamas top with his gene trousers. As a result, his mother began to watch him closely. One day she entered his room without any warning and discovered his problem. He had grown a second penis! His parents did not know that he has been sleeping with their demonic housemaid who has caused this problem. Sex can destroy!

 Sex is very potent and the power contained in it can be compared with atomic energy...The same atomic energy that can generate enough electricity to power a city can also destroy a city

Many years ago, another lady had a prophecy from the Lord that she was going to take the gospel around the world. She was holding on to the prophecy and was walking accordingly until some of her friends began to make fun of her. They teased her about the flatness of her breasts tying it to the fact that it was because she was still a virgin and had not had sexual intercourse with anybody. They said all sorts of rubbish into her ears and unfortunately, she listened. She then met a strange man and went ahead to sleep with him. Now, she is at the MFM headquarters every morning praying, because after sleeping with that man, her vagina closed.

So if you claim to be a child of God and you are still sleeping with anybody before marriage, you are losing so many blessings. Even if you claim that you are doing it because you are about to get married, it is still regarded as a sin in the sight of the Almighty. And to tell you the truth, sex cannot tie down a man. Any man who is truly serious about marriage will not be in a hurry to have sex; he will be willing to wait until after marriage.

God created sex and He had a purpose in mind when He created it. He made it for procreation and companionship in marriage. When sex is had within the confines of marriage, it attracts His blessings, but when done outside it, it brings plenty of problems, woes, tragedy and even death to those involved. It has been said and it is true that "When the purpose of a thing is not known, abuse is inevitable."

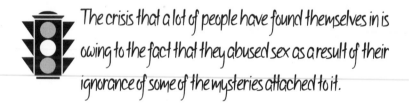

The crisis that a lot of people have found themselves in is owing to the fact that they abused sex as a result of their ignorance of some of the mysteries attached to it.

Chapter
Two

WHEN SEX BECOMES DEADLY:
Reasons Strong Enough To Wait Until Marriage

> It is good for a man not to touch a woman.
> Nevertheless, to avoid fornication, let every
> man have his own wife, and let every woman
> have her own husband.

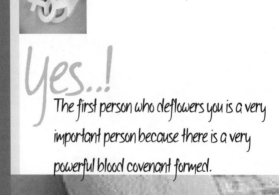

Yes..!

The first person who deflowers you is a very important person because there is a very powerful blood covenant formed.

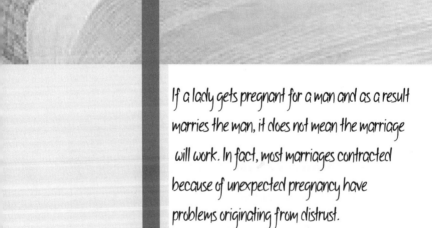

If a lady gets pregnant for a man and as a result marries the man, it does not mean the marriage will work. In fact, most marriages contracted because of unexpected pregnancy have problems originating from distrust.

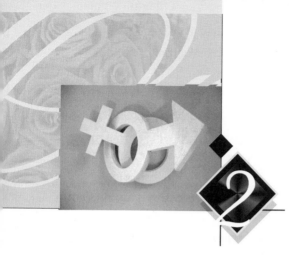

WHEN SEX BECOMES DEADLY: REASONS STRONG ENOUGH TO WAIT UNTIL MARRIAGE

 SEX IS A BEAUTIFUL GIFT FROM GOD AND IT IS RESERVED FOR MARRIAGE ALONE.

GOD HIMSELF CREATED AND DESIGNED SEX for marriage alone. As the creator, he has the master plan for all his creations and He can perfectly fix up whatever is lacking in them physically, spiritually and even emotionally. God knows what every living thing He has created needs for their survival; hence He made adequate provisions for them without any omission. One of those things God created to give balance to the institution of marriage is sex. This is obvious by looking at the male and female anatomy. Sex was already factored into God's design for man from the very beginning.

And so, it was included among the things that He looked at and said was 'very good'. We see confirmation of the intentions of God for sex within marriage in 1 Cor.7.1-5

> *"Now concerning the things whereof ye wrote unto me: It is good for a man not to touch a woman. Nevertheless, to avoid fornication, let every man have his own wife, and let every woman have her own husband. Let the husband render unto the wife due benevolence: and likewise also the wife unto the husband. The wife hath not power of her own body, but the husband: and likewise also the husband hath not power of his own body, but the wife. Defraud ye not one the other, except it be with consent for a time, that ye may give yourselves to fasting and prayer; and come together again, that Satan tempt you not for your incontinency."*

You can see how importantly God placed sex. It was made to fill a big gap, for the avoidance of fornication. That goes to show that sex is basically created for purity. If God had not intended for us to have sexual relationships, He could have created us as androgynous beings (neither feminine nor masculine) which reproduce by an asexual process. But He didn't do that. God instead created us male and female with a strong desire to use and enjoy our sexuality. Despite this, His intention is for us to have access to sex, only by marriage. Any other platform for sex, apart from marriage becomes a divine misplacement which is deadly.

 HAVING SEX WITH A PERSON CREATES A TYPE OF BONDING OR ONENESS WITH THAT PERSON.

The oneness is not just physical; it is also emotional and spiritual in nature. There is a transfer between both parties: good or bad moves from the person to you and then from you to the person. In essence, you have made yourself one flesh with that person.

1 Corinthians 6:15-16

> *"Know ye not that your bodies are the members of Christ? shall I then take the members of Christ, and make them the members of an harlot? God forbid. What? know ye not that he which is joined to an harlot is one body? for two, saith he, shall be one flesh."*

For your life and destiny to be in correct standing, you need to carry out some deliverance exercises to break some soul-ties. You worsen the matter, when you sleep with plenty of them; you fragment your soul into pieces. You will need to gather yourself back together again before things can actually move smoothly. This involves both your marriage and other areas of your life.

There is this prominent man who did not like the Mountain of Fire and Miracles Ministries. But one day something happened to him. His wife was travelling abroad and he escorted her to the airport. After dropping her off at the airport, he picked another lady home and slept with her on his matrimonial bed. Around 1:00a.m. in the middle of the night, however, as he got up to ease himself, he found the lady he brought home lying with her two legs on the wall. He was alarmed because it is believed in Africa that those who sleep with their legs on the wall are witches and have gone for their witchcraft meeting.

He tried to wake her but could not. He shook her

It is not everything that yields to prayer. Some things don't yield to prayer; they yield to repentance... Certain things do not require deliverance; they only submit to character re-arrangement. The same thing goes for fasting.

vigorously but to no avail. He kept trying until 5:00a.m. when he was finally able to wake her up. Apparently, she was just coming back from her witchcraft meeting. Having successfully woken her up, he then chased her away from the house.

The man came to see me that same day. I was surprised when I learnt that he was waiting to see me. He narrated everything that happened. He knew he was in a dilemma and was looking for a fix. I then asked him just to confirm, *"You mean you slept with the woman who slept with her legs on the wall?"* He answered in the affirmative. I then told him plainly. *"Since you slept with her and she is a witch, then you also have become a witch"*. He asked me for the way out and I told him that he would have to embark on a three-day dry fast. He found it difficult to accept since he was used to breakfast along with coffee in the morning. Anyway, since he wanted his freedom, he complied and the Lord showed His mercy, though he still faced the consequences of having sex outside marriage. Things were never the same.

 3 THE BIBLE SAYS WE SHOULD FLEE FROM FORNICATION.

Fornication is sexual intercourse between two people who are not married. It is a divine instruction never to indulge in sex with a person other than your lawful spouse, or else you will bring God's judgment on yourself. The fact that a person has indulged in regular non-marital sex without any seeming repercussion does not mean that judgment will not come. Do not be deceived by that.

The Bible says in Proverb 11:21

> *"Though hand join in hand, the wicked shall not be unpunished: but the seed of the righteous shall be delivered."*

It also says in Galatians 6:7-8

> *"Be not deceived; God is not mocked: for whatsoever a man soweth, that shall he also reap. For he that soweth to his flesh shall of the flesh reap corruption; but he that soweth to the Spirit shall of the Spirit reap life everlasting."*

It is true that we serve a merciful God, but it will be a serious mistake to take Him for granted; especially now that you know the truth.

Hebrews 10:26-27, 31 says:

> *"For if we sin wilfully after that we have received the knowledge of the truth, there remaineth no more sacrifice for sins, But a certain fearful looking for of judgment and fiery indignation, which shall devour the adversaries. It is a fearful thing to fall into the hands of the living God."*

 YOU NEED TO WAIT FOR MARRIAGE BEFORE HAVING SEX IN ORDER TO MAINTAIN YOUR RESPECT.

Sex is worth waiting for; I must confess that to

you. Apart from the fact that it is dirty and unhealthy to be sexually loose, you automatically trade your self-respect. Your sex partners will see you as a cheap and easy-to-catch person. You lose the trust they can have for you, which is why most relationships that involve sex don't lead to marriage. As a lady, men will respect you when you insist on marriage first before sex. And if he says without sex, no marriage; then you let him go or else you will be added to the list of those he has slept with.

 YOU SHOULD WAIT IN ORDER TO HAVE A CLEAR CONSCIENCE AND NO WORRIES OR REGRETS.

When a jilted person takes it too personal to the point of considering suicide or vow never to go into any other relationship, it is due to the fact that she has gotten involved in pre-marital sex. But if you keep yourself from sex a breakdown in the relationship will not cause regret and pain.

As a lady, men will respect you when you insist on marriage first before sex.

● ● ●

33

SEXUAL ACTIVITY IN YOUNG PEOPLE HAS BEEN KNOWN TO ARREST THEIR PSYCHOLOGICAL, SOCIAL AND ACADEMIC DEVELOPMENT.

Studies have shown that those who engage in sex at a young age are generally the bottom performers in class. This reason is strong enough for the young singles to keep off.

 MAJORITY OF 'DECENT' WOMEN CANNOT ENJOY SEX OUTSIDE MARRIAGE.

There are a number of issues that give women worries when they engage in sex outside marriage. For example, having to hide for the fear of being caught or the fear of contracting a disease, etc. This is really too much trouble and there is no enjoyment in that. So it doesn't make sense at all when you have so many causes for anxiety troubling you during the act and thereafter.

 HEAVEN WILL APPLAUD YOU IF YOUR VIRGINITY IS GIVEN TO THE MOST IMPORTANT PERSON IN YOUR LIFE.

That is, your husband or wife. The first person who deflowers you is a very important person because there is a very powerful blood covenant formed. As a lady, heaven can even trust your womb with an unborn prophet or prophetess. Just like our Lord Jesus, the birth of some important figures to God requires a vessel that is chosen, pure and divine. Keeping yourself pure has a spiritual value that goes beyond human comprehension; it could be in form of a divine mandate.

 ### YOU DO NOT MAKE YOURSELF AND YOUR DESTINY SOMETHING THAT PEOPLE TOY WITH.

Sleeping with people outside marriage is to make yourself a toy in the hands of others. Sex is deeper than the physical activity people talk about. It can determine a lot about your future. One of the greatest weapons in the hand of the devil to terminate glorious destinies is sex outside marriage. In order to avoid toiling under a bewitched heaven, avoid pre-marital sex.

 ### WAITING UNTIL MARRIAGE WILL ALLOW YOU TO GROW AS A CHRISTIAN

You cannot grow in grace when you are having sex outside marriage. You will even prevent your own prayers from being answered. The Bible says the prayer of a sinner is an abomination to God, hence you automatically fall into the category of those that pray and can never receive an answer. The only prayer a sinner can pray and get a desirable result to, is the prayer for forgiveness.

YOU NEED TO WAIT IN ORDER TO HAVE A CLEAR HEAD WHEN YOU ARE MAKING IMPORTANT DECISIONS.

Heaven will not tell you anything about marriage when you have already started sleeping with a man or woman and then you want to know if that person is God's will for you or not. The mystery of the Christian faith is that once you accept the Lord Jesus Christ as your saviour, your entire being is handed over to Him on the spot. He becomes the owner of your soul too. Immediately you begin to have illicit sexual affairs with a person, your entire life is involved, most especially your soul. You immediately get disconnected from divine connection and get attached to your sex partner. As such, confusion enters, the calmness and contribution of the Holy Spirit to the decisions you make also gets

As a lady, men will respect you when you insist on marriage first before sex.

disconnected. When it gets this bad, any decision you make at that moment does not involve the backing of heaven. Confusion would have set in and getting things right might be so difficult. The decisions people make at their disconnected period from divine contact are usually destructive.

 YOU NEED TO WAIT IN ORDER TO AVOID UNWANTED PREGNANCY.

Unwanted pregnancy often leads to abortion and this has terrible spiritual implications. There is a spirit known as the spirit of abortion and this causes frustration in the life of any one that commits it, unless he or she cries out for mercy. Anything he or she does will not work because the blood of the aborted babies will be crying out against him/her. If it does work, they will lack a firm foundation and as such, will not last long before collapsing. Such a person needs to repent and go for deliverance to break free.

 UNPLANNED SINGLE PARENTHOOD.

Those that get pregnant from sex outside marriage and choose not to go for abortion, for one reason or the other, become emergency single parents. Unplanned single parenthood will not only make their lives miserable it will also subject the innocent child to an upbringing that causes regret and abuse.

 YOU NEED TO WAIT IN ORDER TO AVOID SEXUALLY TRANSMITTED DISEASES:

My original discipline is Microbiology. We cure sexually transmitted diseases because they are microorganisms. In the 70s, there were only 2 sexually transmitted diseases (STDs) and they were both curable. Now, there are over 25 STDs and several of them are completely incurable. Unfortunately for many people, they are not aware that they have these STDs and they have completely destroyed their womb and reproductive organs. There is a particular STD, which does not show until it blocks the fallopian tubes. Once the fallopian tubes are gone, then forget any thing called conception except by divine intervention. When you tell people to wait for marriage, they feel you do not understand what is going on whereas they are

 One of the greatest weapons in the hand of the devil to terminate glorious destinies is sex outside marriage. In order to avoid toiling under a bewitched heaven, avoid pre-marital sex.

the ones ignorant of the full impact of their actions.

 ### YOU NEED TO WAIT IN ORDER TO AVOID DEATH FROM STDs:

A lot of people have died from sicknesses contracted through sex, and many are presently under the agony of these diseases. Indulging in this criminal act shortens lives; it's like signing up for untimely death. Though there are several ways people have devised for themselves to have 'safe sex'. Despite this, however, casualties have not stopped mounting the queue. For example, while a lot of people know that the condom is only about 90% effective, they are not aware that there are some diseases that can evade the condom barrier.

Also, you cannot really tell who has sexually transmitted diseases. For example, most young teenage girls have what we call Chlamydia. And most of them do not know because a lot of these diseases do not have easily noticeable symptoms. The safest and best thing is to avoid pre-marital sex.

16 ORAL SEX IS NOT SAFE TOO.

Many STDs can be transmitted through oral sex as well. It is even worse. Genital herpes, syphilis, gonorrhea, Chlamydia, HIV etc. can be transmitted through oral sex. When I was working in my laboratory in those days, they brought a man to us that had gonorrhea in the throat. To worsen the case, he had conjunctivitis (popularly called Apollo in Nigeria) in his eyes and someone told him that he could use his urine to cure the conjunctivitis by washing his eye with it. So he started using his gonorrhea infested urine to wash his eyes. As a result, his eyes also caught the infection and he now had gonorrhea in three places: throat, eyes and penis.

17 ABSTINENCE IS THE ONLY 100% METHOD OF PREVENTING UNWANTED PREGNANCIES AND STDS.

As a matter of fact if you do not want to be pregnant or impregnate someone before you marry, then avoid pre-marital sex. There are no other options: avoid sex before marriage. As noted above, the manufacturers of condoms do not give you a 100% guarantee because it could **break** in the process. This can result in unplanned pregnancy that will put you into a hard-to-recover-from dilemma.

 SEPARATION FROM GOD AND STINKING IN THE NOSTRILS OF THE ALMIGHTY.

Habakkuk 1:13a

> *"Thou art of purer eyes than to behold evil, and canst not look on iniquity."*

The eyes of the Lord are too pure to behold sin. If God the Father could turn away His face from Jesus on the cross because the sin of the whole world was upon Him, it shows the seriousness of the matter. The moment a man becomes an object of irritation to the Almighty, it is a big deal. His prayers become rejected; he loses favour, even before men. The fact is that, it takes a second and divine touch for such a person to survive life without opting for suicide. Premarital sex is a killer.

 IT MAY LEAD TO WRONG MARRIAGE.

There are some marriages people had to force themselves into as a result of the outcome of the premarital sex they indulged in.

If a lady gets pregnant for a man and as a result

marries the man, it does not mean the marriage will work. In fact, most marriages contracted because of unexpected pregnancy have problems originating from distrust. Such marriages were done without proper planning, thereby resulting in the lack of proper knowledge of each other. Most of them do not last. Those that seem to be together for a long period never enjoy their moments together.

 ### BARRENNESS AND OTHER GYNECOLOGICAL PROBLEMS CAN RESULT FROM SEXUALLY TRANSMITTED DISEASES.

The straight fact is that you could be a victim of one of the multiple side effects of having a sexually transmitted disease. Even when they get treated, some of them end up giving a permanent scar to their victims. This is avoidable, avoid pre-marital sex.

 ### DESTINY DERAILMENT.

All the devil needs to catch up with someone is to make him or her go off the rails in the issues vital to his or her life. It is like going on an adventure to a clumsy land without a map or compass. The end-result is usually fruitless. In other words, I am saying that it is impossible to be sexually loose and be in good terms with the Almighty. He becomes a stranger over the affairs of your life once you cannot control your sexual urges. God would no longer be responsible for whatever happens to you and as such, you stand the risk of missing your divine destiny. That is a risk which is not worth taking for sex, or for any reason at all.

22 CREATING LADDERS AND OPEN DOORS FOR THE DEMONIC INVASION OF SEXUAL AND OTHER WICKED SPIRITS.

There are spiritual doors through which the devil uses to penetrate people's lives on a daily basis, and sexual organs are a major culprit. Having sex with a person you are not married to is one of the routes that leads to demonic possession by all kinds of evil spirits. This happens when your sex partner is possessed. Now, even if he/she is not possessed, by virtue of the fact that you have successfully defiled

Having sex with a person you are not married to is one of the routes that leads to demonic possession by all kinds of evil spirits.

yourselves, demons can enter. Just as bacteria will invade a dirty place, so also demons will invade a dirty life. Once they come in, they master the environment and then bring in as many other wicked demons as possible. Their presence in a person's life is reflected through many ways: strange sickness, confusion, mistakes and errors, etc. Is it not better to stay clean? Be warned!

 DISTORTION OF THINKING PROCESS AND REVELATION POWERS INVITING THE SPIRIT OF MISTAKE AND ERROR.

Romans 8:5, 14 says:

> *"For they that are after the flesh do mind the things of the flesh; but they that are after the Spirit the things of the Spirit.*
>
> *For as many as are led by the Spirit of God, they are the sons of God."*

We are in the end times and as the bible predicts, the level of evil-doing has been unprecedentedly hiked. And no one seems to have a solution for it. But the children of the most High God are led by His spirit on how to survive the perilous times. If you defile yourself with premarital sex you can never benefit from the promise of the Comforter who has already been sent to us. He guides us and leads us away from the scenes of destruction. The Holy Spirit knows all things; you need Him to survive. Avoid premarital sex.

 SEX OUTSIDE MARRIAGE IS BOTH PSYCHOLOGICALLY DAMAGING AND EMOTIONALLY DANGEROUS BECAUSE IT HAS THE POWER TO TAMPER WITH OUR THOUGHT PROCESSES.

Any individual who engages in premarital sex would eventually begin to reason according to the desires of the flesh rather than following the leading of the Holy Spirit. The desires of the natural man will be strengthened due to the sexual intercourse between the two individuals who are not married.

Premarital sex unfortunately gives the enemy legal ground to enter and toy with a person's life. Spiritually the mind will be attacked, slowly giving way to corruption and deterioration of one's character and personality.

Renewal of the mind through the word of God at this stage becomes seemingly impossible because once the soul is under the bondage of sin; it becomes more gullible and more easily deceived. Spiritual insight and perception is lost, the soul is left in darkness and confusion.

25 TO INCREASE YOUR CHANCE OF HAVING A WONDERFUL AND LASTING MARRIAGE.

By research, people who wait till they are married before they have sex, stand a lower risk of divorcing later. Laying a wrong foundation for your marriage through the avenue of sex leaves a wrong idea about the institution of marriage. Sex cannot make a marriage, as it is not the primary purpose of marriage. Even though 1Cor 7:2 has advised each man or woman to have their spouse to avoid sexual immorality, it does not mean that marriage is all about sex.

The partners who decide to marry because they feel they are sexually compatible, will end up in divorce or separation the moment the marriage is faced with real challenges. Unfortunately by this time, they now come to the realization that they and their spouses had nothing in common.

In addition, if casual sex has been a part of your relationship with the opposite sex, it becomes easy to develop a pattern of shaky relationships, easy breakups, STDs, infidelity, and a general lack of stability in your life.

Abstinence between partners in courtship can help shield them from bitter emotions for one another, in the event that such courtship does not end in marriage.

26 FREEDOM FROM REGRET, HEARTBREAK AND ANGER THAT SEX OUTSIDE MARRIAGE BRINGS.

Humans are emotional beings, who possess the ability to feel love, hatred, anger, bitterness etc. Sex between married couples was designed by the Almighty to strengthen the trust, commitment and relationship existing between them. It also develops a feeling of dependency and vulnerability. This emotional process of giving yourself away to your partner is safer within the bonds of a legal union called marriage.

Abstinence between partners in courtship can help shield them from bitter emotions for one another, in the event that such courtship does not end in marriage. More than 80 percent of couples feel high levels of resentment towards an ex, due to the sexual relationship which existed between them. We should know that sex is one way of expressing or showing commitment to a partner within the bonds of marriage. Now if this is abused by engaging in it outside marriage, certain negative sentiments and emotions are bound to set in.

YOU HAVE COMPLETE PEACE OF MIND WITHIN YOURSELF AND WITH GOD.

1Peter 2:11

> *"Dearly beloved, I beseech you as strangers and pilgrims, abstain from fleshly lusts, which war against the soul;"*

A Christian, even one who has been a believer for years stands the risk of losing the inner peace that accompanies knowing God if he or she begins to engage in sex outside marriage. Premarital sex encourages other forms of terrible behaviour such as indecency, lying, lack of integrity, loss of self control, sexual addiction, pornography, masturbation, etc. It could also lead to bitterness and hardness of heart, loss of contentment, peace, and an overwhelmingly dissatisfied spiritual life.

The sexual lusts which spur and also result from it would have successfully loaded the spirit man of such individuals with so many negative materials, which they find warring within their members.   Christians who find themselves entangled in such a trap often find it hard to pray, read their Bibles, engage in any meaningful spiritual activity or even tell others about Jesus. They are therefore neither at peace with themselves nor with God.

28 EASIER TO BREAK UP (IF NEED BE) IF SEX IS NOT INVOLVED.

The power the Almighty has deposited in sex is one that will remain a mystery to man. Sex has the power to unite two people and bind them to each other even after the deed is done and they have gone their separate ways. Premarital sex has an insatiable and progressively enslaving nature which individuals tend to underestimate. As humans, we are not only sharing bodily fluids; a much deeper and mysterious connection is made with our souls.

Partners who practice abstinence will find it easier to walk away from any unfavourable relationship since there is no deep emotional attachment involved. You must learn to take a bold step of breaking off from any relationship where it is evident that you and your partner are incompatible or the Lord is not leading you to marry such a person. The will power to walk away will still be there. Sex binds the souls of two people, fusing their emotions, feelings and desires. This makes it harder for individuals who have been engaging in premarital sex to leave such a relationship. As a result, the person gets trapped with multiple emotional injuries.

29 WITH-HOLDING SEX IS THE EASIEST WAY TO SEE IF YOUR PARTNER IS ONLY IN IT FOR SEX.

A partner may view courtship as an opportunity of experimenting sex with someone they can trust (whether intentionally or unintentionally). This shouldn't be the case. If you wait till you are married to have sex, you will know for sure that your partner loves you enough to be with you and only you. He or she will trust you in the marriage and can vouch for your faithfulness and integrity when you eventually marry. If you are in a relationship where your partner runs after you demanding sex, once he or she has it, take it that the loophole created can never be filled.

30 THERE IS NO GOING BACK ONCE THE MISTAKE HAS BEEN MADE-

You can't change your past, but you can make a conscious effort to avoid the mistakes that later bring regret in life. If you wait for marriage before you have sex; birth control, abortion, single parenting, STDs, guilt and regret won't be a problem. Even if you breakup before marriage, though heartbroken, you will still have the gift of your virginity to bestow on a more worthy partner that you vow to spend the rest of your life with. No one practicing abstinence has ever become pregnant, contracted an STD or regretted losing their virginity to a less worthy individual, except in the case of rape. Do not be deceived, there is nothing like 'safe sex' outside marriage, as far as Christianity is concerned. The contraceptive pills people use have their own dangerous side effects. Premarital sex also fosters lack of sexual discipline and disharmony in the home as it increases the chances of divorce later. Unfortunately this breakup does not end with the parents. In almost all cases, children from broken homes suffer numerous consequences, which escalate to cause rot and defilement in the society.

 YOU MAY CARRY UNWANTED BAGGAGE LIKE MEMORIES FROM THE PAST EMOTIONAL SCARS AND UNWANTED MENTAL IMAGES CAN DEFILE YOUR THOUGHTS.

The Bible says in Prov 23:7

"For as he thinketh in his heart, so is he:"

You are what you think. The process of sanctification entails different stages whereby the Almighty seeks to correct our thought process. Continuous meditation on a particular issue for a long period of time can actually build a mental stronghold which can hold us captive, if the thoughts are negative. This would not only affect our mental and psychological health by causing depression, fear, pessimism, guilt, worry, anxiety, developing destructive habits such as drinking alcohol, loss of weight (from skipping meals caused by loss of appetite). The images of 'passionate' moments shared together would continuously replay themselves in an individual's mind, serving the sole purpose of defiling the individual. It is even possible for an individual who is married and does not properly deal with his or her thought life in the corridor of prayers to continually replay such dirty memories in his or her mind. This unfortunately is a form of adultery that can occur between couples.

 IT INITIATES A POSSIBLE GENERATIONAL PROBLEM WHICH WOULD EXTEND TO YOUR OFFSPRING.

Exodus 20:5.

> *"Thou shalt not bow down thyself to them, nor serve them: for I the LORD thy God am a jealous God, visiting the iniquity of the fathers upon the children unto the third and fourth generation of them that hate me;"*

The story of Abraham is a classical example of what the consequences of sex outside marriage can do; not only to a man but his unborn generation. Abraham succumbed to the lust of the flesh when he decided to sleep with Hagar, his wife's maid (Genesis 16). That one encounter gave birth to Ishmael who would later become the father of the Arab nation. The Arab nation has remained one of Israel's most bitter enemies till date.

Reuben (Abraham's grandson) lost his birthright, and received a curse from his father because of the same problem of sexual promiscuity. He slept with his father's wife (Genesis 35:22, 49:3-4).

Judah (another grandson of Abraham) slept with his daughter in-law (Genesis 38). David (a descendant of Abraham) committed adultery and murder (2 Samuel 11).

David's son, Amnon, raped his half-sister Tamar (2 Samuel 13). Solomon (another of David's son) married 700 women and had 300 concubines.

Whatever we do in our lifetime will have effect on the unborn generations whether good (Hebrews 7:9-10) or bad (Ezekiel 18:2, Lamentations 5:7).

GOD HIMSELF WILL SUPERVISE YOUR PUNISHMENT FOR DEFILING HIS TEMPLE.

1 Corinthians 3:17-18, 10:8

> *"Know ye not that ye are the temple of God, and that the Spirit of God dwelleth in you? If any man defile the temple of God, him shall God destroy; for the temple of God is holy, which temple ye are."*
>
> *"Neither let us commit fornication, as some of them committed, and fell in one day three and twenty thousand."*

God does not take the issue of fornication lightly at all. It is not the kind of offence which He punishes with just a slap on the wrist. We are the creation of the Almighty. It is only fair to God who made us that we should pattern our lives according to His will. If we decide to go against the perfect plan of God concerning sex and its proper use, we should not be surprised at the consequences which will inevitably follow such action. If you carefully go through the Bible, you would discover that the people and nations that were involved in sexual sins got their full share of lasting punishment and even destruction.

34 LOSS OF VIRGINITY AND ENTERING INTO BLOOD COVENANT OF FIRST SEXUAL PARTNER.

Your virginity is the most prized possession that you can give your partner on your wedding night. Once you lose it, no amount of prayers can bring it back. To lose something so precious in a careless and thoughtless manner shows a high level of irresponsibility on our parts. Careless loss of virginity not only sets us against our Maker but also against ourselves.

As virgins the first individual we have sexual intercourse with brings us into a blood covenant with such a person. Blood is very sacred to the Almighty (Leviticus 17:11) and He does not treat issues concerning it lightly. We all have different family backgrounds, foundations and histories; this leaves us vulnerable to introduce all sorts of foreign demons, spirits, curses and covenants into our lives by that singular act.

35 TURNS GOD'S GREAT GIFT INTO CHEAP AND SELF-CENTERED PLAY THEATRE.

God made the pleasure which comes from sexual intercourse to be enjoyed within the legal bounds of marriage. It is unfair to God and us to enjoy such pleasure that was not created for unmarried people. At first, it may feel like enjoyment but the end result is not palatable. Premarital sex defeats the purpose of courtship, because once sex finds itself in any relationship (whether accidently or intentionally) it will automatically complicate it. Issues such as birth control, unwanted pregnancy, trust, STDs amongst others will begin to occupy your mind. These issues will hinder you from really getting to know the other person thus building a shaky foundation. You will have no personal connection with the person but only physical intimacy.

36 FORMATION OF SOUL TIES THAT MAY TAKE AGES TO BREAK.

Sexual intercourse fuses the spirits of two individuals together. When two elements are fused, they become inseparable. Under God's design for marriage, a man and woman who have become one flesh cannot be separated without suffering great damage and pain or even destruction. When God created the union of marriage, he never intended divorce (Matthew 19:8). Sex was intended for a lifelong union. If you entangle yourself with a person through sex and then decide not to continue the relationship, it can take years before you completely break free from that person. Even then, God's mercy is required for total liberation.

 SEXUAL INTIMACY PRODUCES MORE BROKEN RELATIONSHIPS THAN STRENGTHENED ONES.

Sexual intercourse was designed by God to bind a couple in an exclusive relationship shared with no one else. Often, premature sexual involvement blocks the development of true intimacy because it becomes the focus of the relationship rather than friendship being central to the relationship. If weaknesses and differences have not been thoroughly explored but are discovered after sexual involvement occurs, the partners will find themselves struggling harder to work through problems. An individual may try to convince himself or herself that premarital sex is an innocent effort to ascertain sexual compatibility. God's word is clear about such; premarital sex is fornication and thus a sin.

 MOST MEN DO NOT MARRY THE MOTHER OF THEIR FIRST CHILD PRODUCED THROUGH PRE-MARITAL SEX.

Premarital sex is more common among people who have no idea whatsoever of the great responsibilities that accompany the birth of a child. Premarital sex does more harm than good to oneself and his or her partner. Most men who are faced with the issue of accepting responsibility for an illegitimate child may readily assume the role of a father but not a husband. These men may not feel enough love or affection to marry the mother of their child, as the relationship may not have been a serious one, or one that was never intended to end in marriage. There is also the possibility that the persons involved engaged in a 'one-night-stand' or 'spur-of-the-moment' flings where there are no strings attached and never anticipated the possibility of such meetings producing a child.

 IF YOU HAVE DELIVERANCE ISSUES, YOU WOULD COMPLICATE SUCH.

When you are engaging in premarital sex, it cripples your self control and poisons other virtues.

Proverbs 25:28

> *"He that hath no rule over his own spirit is like a city that is broken down, and without walls."*

Once the walls of the city are breached, its citadel can easily be captured. When you lack self-control, you open the door for Satan to come into your life and commit whatever havoc he wants. The Scriptures describe those controlled by their lusts and who concede to passion with the phrase 'unstable as water'. They tend to become more self-willed, restless, moody and stubborn. Spiritual jewels like humility, gentleness, meekness are stripped away and spoilt.

40 SELF-CONDEMNATION

Sex is one of the most beautiful things you'll ever share with another person. However, the true beauty of it can only be experienced if you share it with the right person. Unfortunately for many, bad decisions and choices have left them with deep emotional scars, which have weakened them physically, spiritually and mentally.

Most people feel remorse after having sex before marriage (especially when it doesn't lead to marriage). This period is often characterized by a feeling of worthlessness and lack of any value, having given out something so precious for nothing. The person feels cheap and used. The regret and guilt of not preserving yourself will keep coming back to haunt you. Self-condemnation can also come into play when such an act involves the conception of a baby.

41 UNNECESSARY STRESS AND ANXIETY

Even the most casual and transitory relationships can forge emotional bonds. How much more a relationship that involves something as deep as sex. Premarital sex brings different issues to light, such as worrying that you're pregnant (*for the females*) or fear of responsibility in fathering a child (*for the males*), fear that you may have contracted an STD (*your partner could have multiple partners*), regret, fear of not finding someone else or fear of committing to someone else, guilt, loss of self-respect, loss of trust for people and depression. Sex before marriage has emotional consequences that can bring long-term pain, grief, and worry, which could in turn escalate into more dangerous health issues such as high or low blood pressure, mental illness, heart problems, or lead to an individual committing suicide. Some of the side effects are unlikely to be discerned or discovered until it is too late.

42 THE RISK OF CONCEIVING ILLEGITIMATE CHILDREN.

A child born out of wedlock is legally regarded as an illegitimate child. The truth of the matter is, whether legitimate or illegitimate, children are a godly heritage and His ideal plan is for every human being to have them within the context of a legally defined union called 'marriage'.

One of the risks associated with having children outside wedlock is the possible risk of the man refusing to take complete responsibilty of the child. Children born out of wedlock have a lot of socio-economic effects on both the parents and the society they reside in. This problem usually brings a form of social stigmatization for the child and the mother within the society. It breeds different types of negative emotions (*anger, bitterness, hatred, etc.*) in the life of the resented mother and child.

In most cases, the lady in question loses her respect within the society (*most especially in this part of the world*) as she is seen as very promiscuous while the child tends to be less successful socially and academically than those who come from intact families.This is because the presence of both parents in the upbringing of a child is very paramount. In the spiritual sense, it creates a polluted foundation for the child, which, if not properly dealt with, could lead to generational curse and bondage.

Sex before marriage has emotional
consequences that can bring long-
term pain, grief, and worry, which
could in turn escalate into more
dangerous health issues

43 EVERY RELATIONSHIP YOU BREAK UP WHERE YOU HAVE HAD SEX CREATES STRONG AND OFTEN UNPLEASANT MEMORIES FOR YOUR WHOLE LIFE.

2Samuel 13:19-20.

> *"And Tamar put ashes on her head, and rent her garment of divers colours that was on her, and laid her hand on her head, and went on crying. And Absalom her brother said unto her, Hath Amnon thy brother been with thee? but hold now thy peace, my sister: he is thy brother; regard not this thing. So Tamar remained desolate in her brother Absalom's house."*

In the passage above, we see Tamar's pain based on her experience. If you read the preceding verses of that chapter, you will find out that the major source of her pain was that Amnon put her out after sleeping with her. The same thing happens when people have sex in a relationship, only to later find their hopes of marriage dashed.

The feelings of betrayal, grief, etc will continue to haunt such a person for the rest of his/her life, except by God's mercy. These unpleasant memories may eventually evolve into psychological and mental disorders which would, in most cases, last for a life time. These memories evolve from the experience a person has gained in the relationship and after the breakup. Some women may never be able to get over the traumatic thoughts that a man slept with them and left them for another woman. It's even worse when the man in question uses marriage to deceive the lady into having sex with him only to later end up marrying another woman. Many people never recover from such experiences and most of them afterwards, live their lives in fear and hatred of themselves, their ex and others around them. This usually brings about overly protection of a person's emotions. Only the mercies of God in this instance can restore the woman back to her normal psychological state.

44 FREEDOM FROM GUILTY CONSCIENCE AND WORRIES.

Acts 24:16

> *"And herein do I exercise myself, to have always a conscience void of offence toward God, and toward men."*

Abstinence from sexual relations when a person is still single would lead to a life free from guilt and worries before God and before man. Guilt and worries resulting from premarital sex come into play when the person realizes the effects of their past sexual escapades and the consequences that may experience, most especially after marriage. They include childlessness due to past abortions, blackmail from ex-boyfriend/girlfriends who are in possesion of incriminating materials such as photos, love letters, etc. that could destroy the person's peace for the rest of their lives etc. In most cases, this guilt and worry would inhibit the person from experiencing true joy in any relationship they find themselves in again.

45 INABILITY TO EXPERIENCE TRUE LOVE.

Anyone who has had sex outside marriage may find it difficult to experience what true love is. Sex outside marriage will never have the capacity of bringing true love to a person. A person can only experience true love when they have accepted the love of God in their lives, and this comes by accepting Jesus Christ as their Lord and Saviour. There are four forms of love: *Eros-* love based on sexual attraction, *Storge-* This type of love is what is found within families. *Philia-* Affectionate type of love, and *Agape*-Unconditional love.

At most times what people term love is actually in the real sense lust (Eros- sexual love) which comes as a result of the desire for sexual gratification. When a person has full knowledge of the type of love (Agape-unconditional love) God shows towards us, only then can the person appreciate and experience true love in any relationship they find themselves in.

 IT CAN RESULT IN SUSPICION THAT DESTROYS TRUST AND LEADS TO LATE OR NO MARRIAGE.

Sex outside marriage has a lot of adverse side effects, suspicions being one of them. Most men and women that have had sex outside marriage find it hard to trust their partners in a relationship. Research has shown that couples that engaged in sex before marriage find it hard to trust each other when they are married, even if they engaged in it with each other! This can be a serious destabilizing factor in marriage, as trust is a vital ingredient in cementing marriage.

A lot of suspicions and negative thoughts will be running through their minds, especially whenever their partners are not with them. Some people can't cope with the fact that their spouse came back an hour later than usual. The next thing that comes to their minds is that maybe 'he or she was with someone else'. There would always be this inner feeling that their partner is unfaithful to them. People like these, because of their past sexual escapades, find it difficult to totally trust their partners. Such people can never experience true peace even when they eventually get married. This lack of trust and suspicion will be a source of conflict, as the other party to the relationship may become fed up with their partners' behaviour. This would eventually result in the break up of the relationship. Constant suspicion on the part of one of the parties in a relationship is what results in constant breakup of relationships that should have led to marriage, thereby leading to late marriage.

 ## 47 IT BREEDS HATRED AND STRIFE.

2Samuel 13:14-15

> *"Howbeit he would not hearken unto her voice: but, being stronger than she, forced her, and lay with her. Then Amnon hated her exceedingly; so that the hatred wherewith he hated her was greater than the love wherewith he had loved her. And Amnon said unto her, Arise, be gone."*

After having sex with their partner outside marriage a person may eventually end up hating such partner, because sex was initiated by God to produce an unconditional love and also strenghten the union between the partners within the context of marriage. The result of this hatred by one party in the relationship would eventually lead to the collapse of the relationship. This would leave the other partner aggrieved and embittered. The resented lover would thereby develop negative emotions towards their ex-lover because of the rejection he/she has received. These emotions may, at most times, develop into strife. The latter effects of this strife may result in the embittered spouse taking vengence on their ex-lover which in some cases may lead to the death of one of the partners, as we have seen in the case of Amnon and Tamar (2Samuel 13) when Absalom decided to take revenge for his sister Tamar after she had been violated by Amnon.

 ATTACKS BY SPIRIT WIFE/HUSBAND DUE TO IMPURITY AND LUST (GENESIS 6:2-4, 1THESSALONIANS 4:3-4).

Sex outside marriage creates a legal ground for demons to enter and take possession of a person's life. This is the reason why so many people find themselves under the control of forces that are beyond there physical comprehension. Spirit husbands and wives, commonly known as Inccubi and Succubi in deliverance ministry, have been since the creation of Adam and Eve. These demonic spirits take control of people's bodies and mostly attack those who are sexually loose. Sexual immorality is one of the doors through which they invade lives. The sexually loose people, who are subject to lust and defilement, are the main toys in the hands of these wicked demons.

The most terrible thing about these attacks from spirit spouses is that it can come in both physical and spiritual ways and a person who has no knowlegde of deliverance would eventually spend their whole life subjected to their control.

 49 AVOIDING UNNECESSARY STRESS.

Sex was designed by God to consist between two emotionally, physically and financially mature persons within the context of marriage. Those who are not married have no business engaging in it. When a person is emotionally, physically and financially mature he or she would be able to successfully cope with all the outcome that result from it. Sex within marriage would help someone avoid unnecessary terrible consequences like anxiety, grief, bitterness and regret which result in mental and emotional stress for couples who are not ready to bear the consequences of their actions.

50 EASIER TO TELL FUTURE PARTNER ABOUT YOUR PAST.

Every relationship should posses a high level of transparency in it. From the inception of every relationship that is intended to lead to marriage, both partners have a duty to disclose any relevant information that may pose a threat to the peace of that relationship. With no shameful past or dark secrets to hide, it is easier for a person to tell their partners about their past.

In the case when a person has lived a loose sexual life in the past (most especially females), where they have had a series of abortions which might have led to their wombs being partially or permanently damaged in the process, or in a situation when one partner caught a veneral disease like gonorrhea or syphilis, it is harder to reveal such information to their partner. In the end, when such secrets are found out, all hell would break loose in such relationships, which may likely result into a breakup.

51 IT LEADS TO A DISTORTED FAMILY LIFE.

This happens after pre-marital sex has resulted into an unplanned parenthood. A man or woman that has had a child or children for one or more different people stands the risk of having a distorted family life. After he or she eventually settles down in marriage, his or her attention would be divided around the scattered children under different roofs of their both parents. It's more headache-giving than it sounds because, as a matter of fact, you have already divided yourself unnecessarily. It could be avoided if you abstain from pre-marital sex.

 52 IT DOWNPLAYS OTHER WAYS OF SHOWING LOVE.

When a relationship is just based on sex, other forms of expression of love would be phased out. Exchange of gifts, going on outings together in open places, regular communication, creating time for fellowship with one another etc, are all ways in which partners can show affection for one another without having sex in their relationship.

Sex may bring two people together, but it would only be temporary. Real love goes beyond sex. It consists of the little ways we show each other that we appreciate each other's uniqueness. When people have a basic knowledge that sex is restricted only within the boundaries of marriage, it will encourage people to create other ways of expressing love towards one another which excludes any form of sexual activities

 ALLOWING YOUR BODY TO BE USED AS A TOOL FOR ENTERTAINMENT BY THOSE WHO PROMISE MARRIAGE, LOVE OR COMMITMENT JUST TO GET SEX

Romans 6:13

> *"Neither yield ye your members as instruments of unrighteousness unto sin: but yield yourselves unto God, as those that are alive from the dead, and your members as instruments of righteousness unto God."*

1Corinthians 3:16

> *"Know ye not that ye are the temple of God, and that the Spirit of God dwelleth in you?"*

Fondling, oral sex, heavy petting and other forms of semi-sexual activities are unlawful uses of a person's body. Any man who promises marriage based on sex is not worth marrying as such a person lacks the fear of God and does not love you as he/she claims to. Notwithstanding, the fact that the man uses such a pickup line for one woman shows that he would simply use it for another woman when he gets tired of the first. In most cases, when a man has been given unrestricted access to a woman's body, it is rare for the relationship to end in marriage. Women should learn to uphold their dignity, keep their bodies holy and say no, to men offering marriage, commitment and love in return for sex.

 ZERO SPIRITUAL GROWTH ON AN EXPRESS WAY TO HELL FIRE.

Isaiah 35:8

> *"And an highway shall be there, and a way, and it shall be called The way of holiness; the unclean shall not pass over it; but it shall be for those: the wayfaring men, though fools, shall not err therein."*

Revelations 21:8

> *"But the fearful, and unbelieving, and the abominable, and murderers, and whoremongers, and sorcerers, and idolaters, and all liars, shall have their part in the lake which burneth with fire and brimstone: which is the second death."*

Sin seperates us from God. When a person has been cut off from the presence of God, the person would experience no spiritual growth. We need the daily presence of the Holy Spirit to help us grow as Christians, but the Spirit of God will only reside in a purified and sanctified body. Only one thing is evident here. Without a regular and consistent spiritual growth as a Christian, such a person is headed for destruction. Failure to repent would eventually guarantee that the

person would end up in hell fire.

55 DAMAGED SELF-ESTEEM.

Using sex as a coping mechanism can create low self esteem, depression and interpersonal problems and this often leads to hyper-sexuality. Some people only see themselves through the eyes of others and feel they have no personal value unless they attach themselves to someone else. Such people are emotionally unstable and are willing to do anything, even going against their own wishes just to find some form of acceptance. The individual would continuously use sex as a means to gain some form of acceptance in trying to find some self worth, which is never going to surface from that direction.

56 IT LEAVES YOU EMPTY AND SEARCHING FOR REAL LOVE.

Anything that will not increase you will only decrease you. Through sexual relationships, people's souls are divided into the lives of others, leaving them spiritually and physically empty. Premarital sex can lead to emotional emptiness, regret, distrust and distress. It always leaves one party to the relationship feeling empty and used and their emotions physically abused and battered. Such issues if not properly addressed may result in a crisis for the individual. Some people, especially ladies tend to engage in sex as a way of satisfying a deep emotional hunger for love and affection. When this is done outside the confines of marriage, the person is unsatisfied after the act and keeps longing for more. Sex cannot be used as a medium of exchange to buy love. You do not need to engage in sex to show that you love someone or to get love from a person.

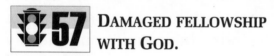 **57** ### DAMAGED FELLOWSHIP WITH GOD.

Isaiah 59:20

> *"And the Redeemer shall come to Zion, and unto them that turn from transgression in Jacob, saith the LORD."*

Premarital sex damages our relationship with God. It cuts a person off from His glorious presence and fellowship with Him is automatically terminated. Such a person will be cut off from many privileges they receive while in fellowship with Christ, such as dreams, visions and mighty revelations. These may all disappear when sin is in place. Men and women make a big mistake when they think they can break the law of God and not suffer the eternal consequences. A person who fails to repent would eventually end up in hell fire.

 ## STRENGTHENING INTERNAL YOKES AND BONDAGES.

Sin gives a foothold for the devil to have a legal ground in a person's life and do whatever he pleases with the person in question. Sin also hinders our complete deliverance. The fact is that as long as a person is still living in sin, especially the sin of fornication, he/she can never be free from any type of bondage he/she is in, no matter how much the person may fast and pray or go for deliverance.

 ## DAMAGED WOMB OR REPRODUCTIVE ORGANS.

STDs like gonorrhea and syphillis (which make a person sterile) and also constant abortions (through pills and operations) due to premarital sex would eventually lead to damaged wombs and reproductive organs. Many men and women eventually have to pay a lifetime price of no children in marriage or worse still, no marriage at all. It would take the mercies of the living God for a woman/man who has a damaged womb/reproductive organ, to ever have any chance of giving birth in life.

Abstinence between partners in courtship can help shield them from bitter emotions for one another, in the event that such courtship does not end in marriage.

60 AVOIDING BIRTH CONTROL SIDE EFFECTS.

Birth control pills have numerous documented side effects such as mood swings, nausea, breakthrough bleeding and breast tenderness. It is wise for you to wait until the right time so that you would not have to "diligently" fight nature by putting off conception with these contraceptive pills. It is better to abstain from pre-marital sex than to try to "eat your cake and have it".

61 TRUE LOVE WILL WAIT AND WILL NOT SUBJECT PARTNERS TO FEAR OF DISEASES, UNWANTED PREGNANCY AND PSYCHOLOGICAL DIFFICULTIES OF PRE-MARITAL SEX.

Delving into pre-marital sex is like opening a can of worms. The repercussion is not palatable. Like I mentioned earlier, with pre-marital sex comes the fear of contracting STDs and unwanted pregnancy. True love would not subject its partner to any of these fears as it is written in I John4:18:

> *"There is no fear in love; but perfect love casteth out fear: because fear hath torment. He that feareth is not made perfect in love."*

In other words, true love waits!

62 IT IS A TRUST DESTROYER.

Trust is the bedrock of any relationship. Once trust is gone or even questionable, the relationship is over. Pre-marital sex puts the participants in a bad shape. It causes people to doubt the fidelity of their intending partner. Anybody who compels his/her partner to pre-marital sex just because he/she isn't in control of his/her sexual desires is not only selfish but is building a faulty foundation for the relationship itself.

63 IT MULTIPLIES SEXUAL DESIRES AND CAN CAUSE SEXUAL ADDICTIONS.

As mentioned above, sex in itself was created by God to be enjoyed by married couples. Pre-marital sex is an invention of the devil, a perversion of God's original plan and a work of the flesh. It doesn't have God's blessing or approval therefore all those who partake of it are at its mercy. The sexual drive is one of the strongest urges in the human being (*second only to self-preservation*). Therefore we are compelled by scripture to put our bodies under subjection (*1 Corinthians 9:27*), and to "*Let not sin therefore reign in your mortal body, that ye should obey it in the lusts thereof".* (**Romans 6:12**). Failure to do so would only make you a slave of your sexual desires. Engaging in pre-marital sex in order to release sexual tension or urge doesn't make things better. It makes things worse. Your giving in to such urges weakens your spirit and kills your resistance to sin thereby enslaving you further. Before you know it, you're no longer in charge.

 TO AVOID CANCER, PELVIC INFLAMMATORY DISEASE AND INFERTILITY.

Genital warts are a sexually transmitted infection (STI). They are soft growths on the skin and mucus membranes of the genitals which can be found on the penis, vulva, urethra, vagina, cervix, and around, and, in the anus. The virus that causes this is called Human Papilloma Virus (HPV). More than 70 different types of it exist. Certain types of HPV can lead to pre-cancerous changes in the cervix, cervical cancer or anal cancer. These are all high-risk types of HPV. The strange part is that though HPV infection around the genitals is common, most people have no symptoms. In women, HPV can spread to areas inside the walls of the vagina and cervix yet they can't easily be seen without special procedures.

Why this is of particular importance is that HPV infection spreads from one person to another through sexual contact involving the anus, mouth, or vagina. You can spread the warts even if you do not see them.

 PRE-MARITAL SEX CAUSES COUPLES-TO-BE TO STOP GETTING TO KNOW EACH OTHER AND FOCUS ON SEX INSTEAD.

There is a reason behind every command of God. Whenever God gives any law, instruction, rule or principle; there is always a very good reason behind it and man is the beneficiary. However, due to ignorance, many choose to go their own way. Sex is one area where human beings have consistently flouted God's laws with impunity. There is an intimacy that results from sexual intercourse owing to the bonding that occurs in its consummation. God made it so to enable couples renew their love and stay close throughout their lifetimes, considering the tumultuous nature that could attach to marriage.

Such intimacy is not meant for unmarried couples. If unmarried couples engage in sex, they will get carried away by the intimacy and forget about learning more about themselves. The human flesh loves pleasure and there is a lot of pleasure in sex. The disadvantage however, is that they will ignore other important things that may debar them from getting married. So if the premise for engaging in pre-marital sex is that you will eventually marry, and then because of sex, you end up not marrying, then the question is: what's the point? The truth is that there is enough time for sex after marriage. The time of courtship will never be repeated, so it is advisable to use it to know your intending spouse in other ways apart from the bed.

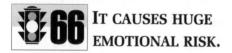 ## IT CAUSES HUGE EMOTIONAL RISK.

As discussed above, sex causes intimacy between partners. This intimacy leads to emotional attachment that can often run very deep. The danger here is that if there is a subsequent break-up, the partners may find it hard to let go of each other. Owing to the fact that their souls have been joined, they may find themselves unable to continue on the journey of life on their own. This can lead to heartbreak, confusion, depression etc. and other consequences such as sex addiction. The dangers for an unmarried couple quite outweigh whatever pleasure is inherent therein.

THE EXPECTANCY THAT COMES WITH WAITING FOR SEX AFTER MARRIAGE DISAPPEARS THE MOMENT THE WOMAN GIVES IN TO SEX BEFORE MARRIAGE.

If divine order is followed and sex is reserved for marriage, it generates expectancy in partners during courtship. They will both be looking forward to it. But the moment the woman gives in, such expectancy is immediately lost. That is the reason why most men tend to dump women after they have had sex with them. Once a man has had sex with a woman before marriage; to him, there is nothing 'special' about the woman anymore. He has been allowed to explore her to the hilt, and as a result, there is nothing to compel him to retain his interest in the woman. Hence, a break-up often occurs.

 IT WOULD BE DIFFICULT TO DISCERN BETWEEN INFATUATION AND TRUE LOVE AS SEX COSTS LOSS OF OBJECTIVITY.

Sex can generate a lot of emotions due to the intimacy involved. These emotions often lead to confusion about the relationship. The partners can no longer think clearly, especially about their future together. Sex blurs the lines such that they cannot really say whether they truly love each other or were simply infatuated. Because they had jumped the gun and gone into sex prematurely, they cannot be sure any more about how deep their feelings are for each other. If they can and actually discover that it was infatuation, they find it hard to break due to the resulting attachment from sex. That is why God reserved sex for marriage, because as a person, you would have been sure of your feelings for the person leading to that commitment. Waiting till marriage ensures that you are absolutely convinced of your choice of partner before sex.

 69 PROBLEMS MASQUERADE MASKED BY PLEASURES OF SEX. AFTER MARRIAGE SUCH FLAWS AND SHORTCOMINGS CAUSE PROBLEMS.

When sex is indulged in during courtship, the couple-to-be tends to ignore other things due to the drive to assuage their sexual desires. The issues that were ignored, overlooked and not properly addressed begin to show up when the realities of marriage set in fully. Courtship is meant to be a time to learn about each other and not to maximize sexual activity. If all you do during courtship is have sex with each other, the issues you will ignore as a result will no longer be ignorable when you are finally married.

70   TEENAGERS, WHO SUBMIT TO PRE-MARITAL SEX EXPERIENCE LOWER SELF-RESPECT, FEAR OF COMMITMENT AND DEPRESSION.

When a person is in the teenage phase, he or she is in the stage of life known as adolescence. He or she has the appearance of an adult but is still developing. Teenagers are not yet adults. As a result of all the hormonal changes going on during this period, there is a drive for sex. However, if they begin to engage in sex during this period, it leads to a lot of emotional problems. That is why marriage is meant for adults only. Lower self-respect, fear of commitment, sexual addiction and depression are some of the consequences of sex in teenagers.

71   SEPARATION FROM THE MINISTRY OF ANGELS WHO DWELL WITH THE HOLY.

The Almighty God is a holy God and as such, he cannot dwell in any form of unholiness.

Deuteronomy 23:14

> *"For the LORD thy God walketh in the midst of thy camp, to deliver thee, and to give up thine enemies before thee; therefore shall thy camp be holy: that he see no unclean thing in thee, and turn away from thee."*

Fornication will drive away God and His angels far away from anyone who is involved in such.

IT DESTROYS PROPER LIFE.

The divine order prescribes sex to be after marriage. Once you engage in it outside marriage, you have broken the divine order and the result will be disorder. It has the ability to turn a lot of things upside down. Many of those who have become permanent deliverance candidates would have no problem if they had not been involved in it.

REJECTION AND DISAPPOINTMENT.

Many people, most especially women, feel they can use sex to buy love. But sex is not the currency of love. Any woman who does so will find herself being used. Once her partners are able to satisfy their sexual urges enough, she finds out that they never truly loved her. Some men use declarations of love as a means of getting a woman to sleep with them. Once they get what they want, they leave. This will cause the woman to suffer the bitter pangs of rejection and disappointment.

TENDENCY OF ADDING INIQUITY TO INIQUITY.

Fornication is a sin, and like all sins, it tends to result in other sins. This happens when the parties involved try to cover it up. Lying to cover up, bitterness due to disappointment, uncontrollable lust leading to further fornication or masturbation, abortion due to unwanted pregnancy etc. are some of the sins that could result from fornication.

 MOST DEMONIC CHILDREN FIND IT EASIER TO COME INTO THE WORLD THROUGH PRE-MARITAL PREGNANCIES, FOR JESUS CHRIST IS NOT THE FOUNDATION OF SUCH UNIONS BUT SEXUAL SINS.

Whenever any child is born out of wedlock, such a child has already started life on a deficit. This is because marriage is the proper spiritual foundation for sex. A child who does not have the benefit of a proper foundation will be open to manipulation from the kingdom of darkness. Most demonized children from the womb are the agents of everlasting sorrow to their parents and societies. There is no way a demonized child can give joy to his or her parents. Such children come easily when they are products of sex outside marriage as their faulty foundation gives the devil a leeway into their lives.

 PERSONS WHO PRACTICE PRE-MARITAL SEX ARE MORE LIKELY TO HAVE EXTRAMARITAL AFFAIRS AS WELL.

When a person engages in sex before marriage, he or she has shown by such an act a lack of self-control. Even after marriage, the lack of self-control will lead to extra marital affairs when problems occur with his or her spouse. Without even having problems, he or she will tend to have affairs because of the negative habit.

 IT CAN LEAD TO UNHEALTHY MEMORIES AND COMPARISONS IN MARRIAGE.

When a person has had sex before marriage, the memories of the relationship will tend to linger after marriage. If there are problems in the marriage, there will be a tendency to compare past sexual partners with his or her spouse. This can lead to extra-marital affairs and if not nipped in the bud, the collapse of the marriage. This is a serious case, and it can happen to anyone in life. When a man or a lady has had sex with 10 people for example, there is the possibility that one of those 10 can perform so well in the act. This experience will be stored into the brain of the person; it will later become a problem for him or her if after marriage he/she discovers that the present partner is not as active as the other sex partner in the past. Naturally, everyone will love to have something better than the previous and if peradventure, the partner cannot meet up to his or her expectations sexually, then the problem begins.

 IF THE TRUMPET SOUNDS WHILE IN THE ACT YOU WILL NOT MAKE HEAVEN.

Just as it is written in the Scripture *"that the son of man cometh like a thief in the night"*. If when he comes, you were caught in the act, it will be so terrible as there will be no room for a quick repentance that can save you from going straight to hell.

 YOU MAY THEREAFTER INITIATE A PROGRAMME OF POVERTY FOR YOUR ENTIRE LIFE.

Just like the saying *"if you fail to plan, you are planning to fail"*. Sex is sweet, sex is good, but it must be with your life partner and that can happen only after you have been married to each other. If all a man can think of doing always and

If all a man can think of doing always and at any point in time is all sex, then he is planting a seed of poverty that will grow and germinate. Premarital sex has the ability to convert a man's life to a fruitless tree.

●　●　●

at any point in time is all sex, then he is planting a seed of poverty that will grow and germinate. Premarital sex has the ability to convert a man's life to a fruitless tree. And like what happened to the tree that Jesus saw when He was hungry and wished to pluck fruit from, only to discover that there is none to pluck. The tree was cursed instantly and that was the end. The same will be the lot of anyone who allows premarital sex to render his *or* her destiny to a state of permanent fruitlessness. Such a person will be counted as a wasted investment by heaven and will receive a divine curse.

 YOU MAY ATTRACT A CURSE UNDER WHICH YOU WILL LABOUR FOR THE REST OF YOUR LIFE   FROM PARENTS OF PARTNERS.

There are different ways of looking at this point. One, if you are from a very innocent background and your foundation is so pure and was not polluted, you are fortunate. But if you just decide to join yourself to a guy or lady whose foundation had been cursed, you will automatically share in the curse that is running after your sex partner, since sex turns two to become one. The second angle to this point is when you attract curses to yourself from your partner's parents. How? If you disappoint their child by refusing to marry him or her because you already had access to him or her sexually, and you don't feel like continuing in the relationship.

 81 SEXUALLY ACTIVE BOYS ARE MORE THAN TWICE LIKELY TO HAVE DEPRESSION AND EIGHT TIMES MORE LIKELY TO ATTEMPT SUICIDE, COMPARED WITH NON-SEXUALLY ACTIVE ONES.

Allow me to repeat that sex is more than a physical thing; there are very serious spiritual and emotional dimensions to it. Research has shown that boys who engage in sex are more than twice likely to have depression and eight times more likely to attempt suicide than non-sexually active boys due to their inability to handle the emotions that bombard them as a deluge because of their sexual activity.

Abstinence between partners in courtship can help shield them from bitter emotions for one another, in the event that such courtship does not end in marriage.

YOU MAY BECOME AN AGENT OF BAD INFLUENCE.

When you engage in sex outside marriage, you can influence a lot of people into following your footsteps including friends, neighbours, siblings, colleagues, etc. People who are easily impressionable or who are struggling to ensure that they do not fall short can be easily tempted by your example. This is very bad as you become responsible for their fall. There is a curse attached to this as we see in Matthew 18:6:

> *"But whoso shall offend one of these little ones which believe in me, it were better for him that a millstone were hanged about his neck, and that he were drowned in the depth of the sea."*

83 MOST CONTROVERSIAL CHILDREN BORN THROUGH PRE-MARITAL SEX DO NOT LIVE LONG, AND IF THEY DO, ARE NOT PERFECTLY CARED FOR AND LOVED BY BOTH PARENTS.

Controversy can result very easily when a child is conceived outside marriage. The question of paternity as well as the shame and gossip associated with the child can lead to neglect, resulting in death. Even if the child lives long, because of the controversy surrounding him opr her, he or she will not receive proper care and attention from both parents. This can introduce trauma into the life of such a child.

84 MOST CHILDREN BORN THROUGH PREMARITAL SEX ARE ALREADY IN THE COVENANT OF FORNICATION, AND THEY WILL NEED DELIVERANCE SO AS NOT TO FOLLOW THE STEPS OF THEIR PARENTS.

The power of heredity is very strong. Research has shown that children get all their characteristics through their parents and this is passed from generation to generation through DNA. The same thing applies spiritually as well.

Hebrews 7:9-10

> *"And as I may so say, Levi also, who receiveth tithes, payed tithes in Abraham. For he was yet in the loins of his father, when Melchisedec met him."*

We see a very clear example given above. The tribe of Levi who were yet unborn when Abraham paid tithe to Melchisedec were said to have paid the tithe while still in Abraham, and as a result, was appointed to collect tithes years later. A child born out of fornication will have inherited that spirit and will need deliverance so that he or she does not begin to pay for the sins of his or her parents.

85 SEX DECLINES IN FREQUENCY AFTER THE HONEYMOON.

Owing to the fact that the couple has explored each other prior to marriage, there will be less passion for sex due to reduced excitement. It is best to save sex for marriage so as to heighten the anticipation and keep the frequency stable in the marriage.

86 COUPLES WHO DELAY SEX UNTIL MARRIAGE HAVE MORE STABLE AND HAPPIER MARRIAGES THAN THOSE WHO HAVE PRE-MARITAL SEX.

When a couple waits for marriage before having sex, they will be saved a lot of heartbreak that those who engage in it may face. As a result, they will have more stable and happier marriages.

87 ABSTINENCE COSTS NOTHING AND HAS NO SIDE EFFECTS.

While many people think sex is cheap, it is not. The cost of sex is unknown by both parties when engaged in, but it is potentially unlimited and can send a person's destiny into bankruptcy. A lot of people try to contain the possible fallout from sex by using various forms and combinations of contraceptives. However, the truth remains that almost all contraceptives have one negative side effect or the other on a person's health. Abstinence on the other hand costs nothing and has no side effects. All those myths being circulated about the effects of not having sex on a woman's womb and childbirth have no medical backing. For your own good, it is better to abstain.

88 TEEN GIRLS WHO ABSTAIN FROM SEX UNTIL THEY ARE OLDER, AND LIMIT SEXUAL PARTNERS TO LATER IN LIFE, ARE LESS LIKELY TO DEVELOP CERVICAL CANCER OR BECOME INFERTILE.

There are quite a number of sexually transmitted diseases (STDs) which a person is exposed to when he or she engages in sex. Women are more susceptible due to the make-up of their reproductive system. The vagina is porous and has cracks in it. This allows for the secretion of fluid to lubricate it during intercourse. Because of this, women can contact diseases easily as the pathogens pass through these cracks and get into her system.

Teenage girls are at a higher risk due to the fact that their reproductive systems are still developing. This makes the effects of any STDs on them more devastating. Some STDs are progressive i.e. they move from stage to stage, becoming more deadly at each successive stage. This can lead to cervical cancer or infertility for them later in life. It is therefore advisable for teenage girls to wait till later in life i.e. when they get married, before engaging in sex.

ALSO, CHILDREN BORN TO YOUNG PARTNERS WHO ARE NOT MARRIED MIGHT SUFFER PHYSICAL, MENTAL OR SEXUAL ABUSE.

When children are born to young people who are not ready for marriage or parenting, such a child is at risk for abuse. Whichever parent is responsible for the upbringing of the child is likely to transfer her frustration about conditions to the child, or neglect the child if a man. This can lead to physical and mental abuse. Also, due to economic pressures and the lack of a partner to join in bringing up the child, the responsible parent may have to leave the child for very long periods because of work. This can lead to sexual abuse from family members or neighbours. The number of such cases has been on the rise and it is believed that this is caused by young couples who engage in unprotected premarital sex that are not prepared to rear children.

90 HAVE TIME TO BUILD A STRONG FRIENDSHIP.

When partners abstain from sex, it gives them time to know each other better and become good friends. Jumping into bed with each other takes up time and prevents them from building friendship. Sex is very addictive and has the potential to make itself the focus of a relationship.

91 EASIER TO PAY ATTENTION TO A PARTNER'S FEELINGS.

When you abstain from sex, you will pay more attention to your partner. You will take time to notice his or her preferences, eccentricities and idiosyncrasies. This will help you know your partner better. Some people think sex is the way to know their partners better. But sex will only help you to map out the person's body. Man is a spirit being and the body is simply a residence for the spirit. So if you only know a person's body, then you do not really know the person. It is like knowing a person's house and claiming to know the person. You can know a residence without knowing the person who lives inside. Paying attention to your partner is one of the best ways to truly know him or her.

92 IT SHOWS MATURITY WHEN YOU ABSTAIN.

One of the signs of maturity is discipline. The ability to abstain from sex is one of the greatest acts of self-control, a person can exhibit. It shows that the person is truly a grown up. If you cannot discipline yourself with regards to sex, you will be opening up your destiny to the devil for free access.

93 THE RELATIONSHIP MAY LAST LONGER IF SEX IS SUBTRACTED FROM IT.

A lot of men who are very persistent about having sex in a relationship often end up being bored with the woman after they have engaged in it. However, if there is no sex, the man will be forced to assess the woman from another view. It does not necessarily guarantee that the relationship will last longer but will ensure that the woman does not end up feeling used and dumped, especially if the man decides to break it up.

94 A CHANCE TO LEARN ABOUT COMMITMENT.

When sex is left out of a relationship, it is a test of true commitment. It will help the partners develop commitment. They will see what it really takes to build a relationship when the distraction of sex is out of the way. When two people are able to remain together for a long time without having sex with each other, then they can be said to have developed a high level of commitment and are ready for marriage.

GOOD ROLE MODEL FOR FRIENDS.

When you abstain from sex, you become a good role model for your friends, as well as family, neighbours, etc. They will be encouraged by your example to control themselves. There is a fallacy that it is impossible to remain single without having sex. When you prove this wrong by your example, others around you will want to tow the same path and keep themselves pure as well

SEX MAY BE MORE SPECIAL IF YOU WAIT.

If you wait for marriage before having sex, it can be more special. Rushing into it prematurely can take away the pleasure which God put in it. It can be painful, coupled with the fact that there will be a tendency to hide for fear of being discovered. These put unnecessary stress on the entire experience. You have the rest of your life after marriage to have sex, so there is no need to rush.

 SEX IS IMPORTANT ENOUGH TO THINK CAREFULLY ABOUT.

Giving the deep spiritual, physical and emotional impact sex has, it is necessary that you take time to think about it before going into it. There is a popular maxim: *"If it feels right, do it"*. The truth however is that what feels right may not always be right. Feelings are a product of emotions and emotions can be very unstable. This is because they can easily be affected by hormones, the environment or even previous activities or encounters you have had. Making a decision on something as important as sex on the basis of how you feel is not right. This is the reason why a lot of people tend to regret their first sexual encounter, because they find out that the love they imagined they had was flitting. Sex is too important for you to just *"go with the flow"*. You need to think about it and consider the consequences before going into it.

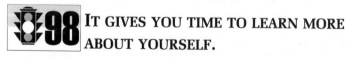 **IT GIVES YOU TIME TO LEARN MORE ABOUT YOURSELF.**

When you rush into sex at a young age, you put

yourself at a great disadvantage. A lot of people are still discovering themselves when they decide to begin having sex. Doing so will only make things more complicated for the person. It is important that you know who you are before you join yourself to another through sex.

 IT GIVES YOU THE CHANCE TO LEARN THE DIFFERENCE BETWEEN LOVE AND SEX.

A lot of people confuse love and sex. They equate them with each other and see sex as a way of expressing love. It is indeed, but only for married couples. There are so many other ways to express love other than sex. However, if you rush into sex, you may not be able to understand the difference. Sex cannot breed love. It can only help to renew love for married couples. One of the most rotten lines that have been used to seduce ladies is: *"If you love me, prove it"*. The truth is that if that man loves you, he will be patient enough to wait for it.

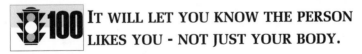 **IT WILL LET YOU KNOW THE PERSON LIKES YOU - NOT JUST YOUR BODY.**

When your partner is able to wait for you, it proves he or she likes you truly and he or she is not just after your body. Marriage is a lifetime commitment and that is why sex is reserved for it. When you have sex outside marriage, there is every possibility that your partner is simply using you to assuage his or her sexual appetite. If he or she can wait till marriage, it proves that he or she truly loves you.

Chapter

Three

THE AFTER EFFECTS
OF PREMARITAL SEX;
Sexually Transmitted Diseases

Sex cannot breed love. It can only
help to renew love for married couples.

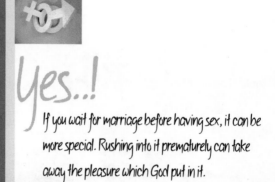

Yes..!

If you wait for marriage before having sex, it can be more special. Rushing into it prematurely can take away the pleasure which God put in it.

When your partner is able to wait for you, it proves he/she likes you truly and he/she is not just after your body.

THE AFTER EFFECTS OF PREMARITAL SEX; SEXUALLY TRANSMITTED DISEASES

◆ **BACTERIAL VAGINOSIS** (BV): The vagina normally contains mostly "good" bacteria, and fewer "harmful" bacteria. BV develops when there is an increase in harmful bacteria. In other words, BV is associated with an imbalance in the bacteria that are normally found in a woman's vagina and it is the most common vaginal infection in women of childbearing age. There are some activities or behaviours that upset the normal balance of bacteria in the vagina and put women at increased risk. They are:

❖ Having a new sex partner or multiple sex partners

❖ Douching: cleaning of the body by squirting water.

Women with BV may have an abnormal vaginal discharge with an unpleasant odour. Some women report a strong fish-like odour, especially after intercourse. Discharge, if present, is usually white or gray; it can be thin. Women with BV may also feel a burning during urination or itching around the outside of the vagina, or both. However, most women with BV report no signs or symptoms at all which makes it more dangerous. There are some serious risks from BV. Having BV can increase a woman's susceptibility to HIV infection if she is exposed to the HIV virus. It also increases the chances that an HIV-infected woman can pass HIV to her sex partner and is also associated with an increase in the development of an infection following surgical procedures such as a hysterectomy or an abortion.

◆ **CHANCROID** is a bacterial disease that is spread only through sexual contact and it is a risk factor for contracting the HIV virus. Within 1 day - 2 weeks after getting chancroid, a person will get a small bump in the genitals. The bump becomes an ulcer within a day of its appearance. That is, chancroid causes ulcers, usually of the genitals. Swollen, painful lymph glands, or inguinal buboes, in the groin area are often associated with chancroid. **If left untreated, chancroid may facilitate the transmission of

HIV.

◆ **CHLAMYDIA** is a common sexually transmitted disease (STD) caused by the bacterium, *Chlamydia trachomatis*, which can damage a woman's reproductive organs and cause infertility if not treated in time. It can be transmitted during vaginal, anal, or oral sex. The danger with it is that symptoms of chlamydia are usually mild or absent and serious complications that cause irreversible damage, including infertility, can occur "silently" before a woman ever recognizes a problem. Chlamydia also can cause discharge from the penis of an infected man. Any sexually active person can be infected with Chlamydia. The greater the number of sex partners, the greater the risk of infection. Because the cervix (opening to the uterus) of teenage girls and young women is not fully mature and is probably more susceptible to infection, they are at particularly high risk for infection if sexually active. Since Chlamydia can be transmitted by oral or anal sex, men who have sex with men are also at risk for Chlamydia infection. Its major havoc is INFERTILITY in both male and female infected person.

◆ **DONOVANOSIS IS AN UNCOMMON BACTERIAL SEXUALLY TRANSMITTED INFECTION (STI). IT CAN BE PREVENTED BY ABSTAINING FROM PRE-MARITAL SEX.** People with donovanosis usually notice one or more fairly painless ulcers or nodules on the genitals, or around the anus or mouth. Without treatment, these will increase in size. Other bacteria can infect these sores, causing them to become painful and distressing with an unpleasant smell. Symptoms generally appear from 3 to 40 days after infection. Occasionally symptoms may take as long as a year to develop. Donovanosis is contagious even when there are no noticeable symptoms.

◆ **GONORRHEA** is a common STI and anyone who has any type of sex can catch gonorrhea. The infection can be spread by contact with the mouth, vagina, penis, or anus. The bacteria grow in warm, moist areas of the body, including the tube that carries urine out of the body (urethra). In women, the bacteria may be found in the reproductive tract (which includes the fallopian tubes, uterus, and cervix). The bacteria can even grow in the eyes. You are more likely to develop this infection if you: have multiple sexual partners, have a partner with a past history of any sexually transmitted infection, etc. Symptoms of gonorrhea usually appear 2 - 5 days after infection, however, in men, symptoms may take up to a month to appear. Some people do not have symptoms. They may be completely unaware that they have caught the infection, and therefore do not seek treatment. This increases the risk of complications and the chances of passing the infection on to another person.

◆ LYMPHOGRANULOMAVENEREUM (LGV) is an STD that primarily infects the lymphatic nodes. It is a chronic (long-term) infection of the lymphatic system caused by three different types of the bacterium *Chlamydi,a trachomatis* and the bacteria spread through sexual contact. LGV is more common in men than women and the main risk factor is being HIV-positive. Its symptoms can begin a few days to a month after coming in contact with the bacteria. Some of its symptoms include blood or pus from the rectum (blood in the stools), drainage through the skin from lymph nodes in the groin, painful bowel movements (tenesmus), small painless sore on the male genitals or in the female genital tract, etc.

◆ MYCOPLASMA GENITALIUM. This is another delicate STD that is transmitted between partners during unprotected sexual intercourse. Some of its various symptoms are: Urethritis (in men), discharge (both sexes), burning while urinating (both sexes), arthritis/reactive arthritis (mostly men), vaginal itching (women), pain during intercourse (women), etc. In the long term, mycoplasma genitalium is suspected to cause pelvic inflammatory disease (PID).

◆ **SYPHILIS** is an STD that has often been called "the great imitator" because so many of the signs and symptoms are indistinguishable from those of other diseases. The transmission of the organism occurs during vaginal, anal, or oral sex. Many people infected with syphilis do not have any symptoms for years, yet remain at risk for late complications if they are not treated. It grows in stages: primary and secondary stages. The primary stage of syphilis is usually marked by the appearance of a single sore (called a chancre), but there may be multiple sores. The time between infection with syphilis and the start of the first symptom can range from 10 to 90 days (average 21 days).

The chancre is usually firm, round, small, and painless. It appears at the spot where syphilis entered the body. The chancre lasts 3 to 6 weeks, and it heals without treatment. However, if adequate treatment is not administered, the infection progresses to the secondary stage. Skin rash and mucous membrane lesions characterize the secondary stage. This stage typically starts with the development of a rash on one or more areas of the body. The rash usually does not cause itching. Sometimes rashes associated with secondary syphilis are so faint that they are not noticed. In addition to rashes, symptoms of secondary syphilis may include fever, swollen lymph glands, sore throat, patchy hair loss, headaches, weight loss, muscle aches, and fatigue. The signs and symptoms of secondary syphilis will resolve with or without treatment, but without treatment, the infection will progress to the latent and possibly late stages of disease. In the late stages of syphilis, the disease may subsequently damage the internal organs, including the brain, nerves, eyes, heart, blood vessels, liver, bones, and joints.

◆ **TREPONEMATOSIS ENDEMIC.** It is also known as treponemiasis and traditionally refers to the group of non-venereal diseases (including endemic syphilis). Patients with treponematosis may have rash or lesions (wounds) that either do not heal or that continue to spread and its later stages may present with various skin, bone, and joint manifestations. At the primary stage, the wounds are painless, white, mucinous ulcers within the oral cavity, where they may be overlooked. Late in the course of disease, it may lead to bone deformities. Much of the transmission is thought to be from mouth-to-mouth contact or from shared eating utensils or drinking cups.

◆ **PUBIC LICE.** Pubic lice are small, six-legged creatures that infect the pubic hair area and lay eggs. Pubic lice are known as *Phthirus pubis* and they usually spread during sexual activity. Almost anyone with pubic lice will have itching in the area covered by pubic hair (it often gets worse at night). This itching may start soon after getting infected with lice, or it may not start for up to 2 - 4 weeks after contact. Other symptoms are skin reaction that is bluish-gray in colour, sores (lesions) in the genital area owing to bites and scratching, etc.

◆ **SCABIES**. Scabies is a well-known infection that results in a particularly relentless and devastating itch that starts out slowly and increases in severity over time. Direct skin-to-skin contact is the mode of transmission. Scabies mites are very sensitive to their environment. They can only live off of a host body for 24-36 hours under most conditions. Transmission of the mites involves close person-to-person contact of the skin-to-skin variety. It is hard, if not impossible, to catch scabies by shaking hands, hanging your coat next to someone who has it, or even sharing bedclothes that had mites in them the night before. Sexual physical contact, however, can transmit the disease. In fact, sexual contact is the most common form of transmission among sexually active young people, and scabies has been considered by many to be an (STD).

◆ CANDIDIASIS VULVOVAGINAL is an infection of the vagina's mucous membranes caused by a type of fungus known as *Candida albicans*. The Candida species of fungus is found naturally in the vagina, and is usually harmless. However, if the conditions in the vagina change, the infection could come up. Predominant symptoms are vulval itching, abnormal vaginal discharges, dyspareunia, dysuria, and odour.

◆ AMEBIASIS: It is an infection of the intestines caused by the parasite *Entamoebahistolytica* which can live in the large intestine (colon) without causing disease. Sometimes however, it invades the colon wall, causing colitis, acute dysentery, or long-term (chronic) diarrhoea. The infection can also spread through the blood to the liver and rarely, to the lungs, brain, or other organs. It is spread through food or water contaminated with stools. This contamination is common when human waste is used as fertilizer. It can also be spread from person to person – particularly by contact with the mouth or rectal area of an infected person. It can thus be transmitted through oral and anal sex. The symptoms could be mild or severe from abdominal cramps, diarrhoea, fatigue, excessive gas, rectal pain while having a bowel movement (tenesmus), unintentional weight loss to severe symptoms such as abdominal tenderness, bloody stools, fever, vomiting, etc.

◆ **CRYPTOSPORIDIUM** is a microscopic parasite that causes the diarrheal disease cryptosporidiosis. Both the parasite and the disease are commonly known as "Crypto." There are many species of *Cryptosporidium* that infect humans and animals. The parasite is protected by an outer shell that allows it to survive outside the body for long periods of time and makes it very tolerant to chlorine disinfection. Some of its symptoms are frequent watery diarrhoea, nausea, vomiting, abdominal cramps, low-grade fever, etc. Cryptosporidium infection can thus be spread in several different ways from contaminated food and water, from animal-person contact, and via person-person contact. No safe and effective treatment has been successfully developed to combat cryptosporidiosis.

◆ **GIARDIASIS.** It is also called **beaver fever** and it is a diarrheal or **diarrhoea** (the condition of having three or more loose or liquid bowel movements per day) infection of the small intestine. There are multiple modes of transmission, including person-to-person, water-borne, and venereal. Some of its risk factors are exposure to a family member with giardiasis, institutional (*day care or nursing home*) exposure and unprotected anal sex. Its symptoms are abdominal pain, diarrhoea, gas or bloating, headache, loss of appetite, low-grade fever, nausea, swollen or distended abdomen, vomiting, etc. The time between being infected and developing symptoms is 7 - 14 days and the acute phase lasts 2 - 4 weeks.

◆ **TRICHOMONIASIS.** It is a sexually transmitted infection caused by the parasite *Trichomonas-vaginalis and it is found all over the world. It is* spread through sexual contact with an infected partner through penis-to-vagina intercourse or vulva-to-vulva contact. The disease can affect both men and women, but the symptoms differ between the two groups. In women, for instance, some symptoms may include discomfort with intercourse, itching of the inner thighs, vaginal discharge (thin, greenish-yellow, frothy or foamy), vaginal itching, vulva itching or swelling of the labia, vaginal odour (foul or strong smell), etc. In men, symptoms include a burning after urination or ejaculation, itching of urethra, slight discharge from urethra, etc.

◆ **CYTOMEGALOVIRUS:** It is abbreviated as CMV and it is a common virus that can infect almost anyone. Most people don't know they have CMV because it rarely causes symptoms. Once a person has had a CMV infection, the virus usually lies dormant (or inactive) in the body, but it can be reactivated. The fact is that, once infected with CMV, your body retains the virus for life. The virus is more likely to be reactivated and cause serious illness in people who have weakened immune systems due to illness. The symptoms of a CMV infection vary depending upon the age and health of the person who is infected, and how the infection occurred. CMV can cause serious infections in people who have received organ transplants or those whose immune systems are weakened. In someone with AIDS or HIV, CMV infection may involve the lungs, nervous system, gastrointestinal tract, and the eye, sometimes causing blindness. Anyone with a new or past CMV infection can transmit the virus to others, even if he or she isn't showing any symptoms. But transmission usually requires fairly close contact; the virus can be spread through saliva, breast milk, vaginal fluids, semen, urine, and stool. It also can be present in blood products and donated organs, causing infection after a blood transfusion or organ transplantation. There's no cure for CMV.

◆ **EPSTEIN BARR VIRUS.** It is frequently referred to as EBV. When infection with EBV occurs during adolescence or young adulthood, it causes infectious mononucleosis 35% to 50% of the time. Symptoms of infectious mononucleosis are fever, sore throat, and swollen lymph glands. Sometimes, a swollen spleen or liver involvement may develop. Heart problems or involvement of the central nervous system occurs, though rarely. Although the symptoms of infectious mononucleos is usually resolved in 1 or 2 months, EBV remains dormant or latent in a few cells in the throat and blood for the rest of the person's life.

Periodically, the virus can reactivate and is commonly found in the saliva of infected persons. This reactivation usually occurs without symptoms of illness. EBV also establishes a lifelong dormant infection in some cells of the body's immune system. A late event in very few carriers of this virus is the emergence of Burkett's lymphoma and nasopharyngeal carcinoma, which are two rare cancers.

The transmission of EBV requires intimate contact with the saliva (found in the mouth) of an infected person. Transmission of this virus through the air or blood does not normally occur. The incubation period, or the time from infection to appearance of symptoms, ranges from 4 to 6 weeks. Persons with infectious mononucleosis may be able to spread the infection to others for a period of weeks. However, no special precautions or isolation procedures are recommended, since the virus is also found frequently in the saliva of healthy people. In fact, many healthy people can carry and spread the virus intermittently for life. These people are usually the primary reservoir for person-to-person transmission. For this reason, transmission of the virus is almost impossible to prevent. Hence, kissing alone can make someone a victim of EBV.

◆ **Hepatitis.** This is swelling and inflammation of the liver. It is not a condition, but is often used to refer to a viral infection of the liver. Hepatitis may start and get better quickly (acute hepatitis), or cause long-term disease (chronic hepatitis). In some instances, it may lead to liver damage, liver failure, or even liver cancer. How severe hepatitis is depends on many factors, including the cause of the liver damage and any illnesses you have. There are causes and risk factors for different types of hepatitis.

TYPES OF HEPATITIS

Hepatitis A is inflammation (irritation and swelling) of the liver from the hepatitis A virus. The hepatitis A virus is found mostly in the stools and blood of an infected person about 15 - 45 days before symptoms occur and during the first week of illness. Symptoms will usually show up 2 - 6 weeks after being exposed to the hepatitis A virus. They are usually mild, but may last for up to several months, especially in adults. Some symptoms are dark urine, fatigue, itching, loss of appetite, low-grade fever, nausea and vomiting, pale or clay-coloured stools, etc. You can catch Hepatitis A if:

❖ You eat or drink food or water that has been contaminated by stools (faeces) containing the hepatitis A virus (fruits, vegetables, shellfish, ice, and water are common sources of the hepatitis A virus).

❖ You come in contact with the stool or blood of a person who currently has the disease.

❖ A person with hepatitis A does not wash his or her hands properly after going to the bathroom and touches other objects or food.

❖ You participate in sexual practices that involve oral-anal contact.

Hepatitis B. This is irritation and swelling (inflammation) of the liver due to infection with the hepatitis B virus (HBV) and it can be spread through having contact with the blood, semen, vaginal fluids, and other body fluids of someone who already has the infection. After someone first become infected with the hepatitis B virus:

❖ There may be no symptoms.

❖ The person may feel sick for a period of days or weeks.

❖ The person may become very ill (called fulminant hepatitis).

If your body is able to fight off the hepatitis B infection, any symptoms that you had should go away over a period of weeks to months. Some people's bodies are not able to completely get rid of the hepatitis B infection. This is called chronic hepatitis B. Many people who have chronic hepatitis B have few or no symptoms. They may not even look sick. As a result, they may not know they are infected. However, they can still spread the virus to other people.

Hepatitis C. The infection is caused by the hepatitis C virus (HCV). People who may be at risk for hepatitis C are those who:

❖ Have been on long-term kidney dialysis.

❖ Have regular contact with blood at work (for instance, as a health care worker).

❖ Have unprotected sexual contact with a person who has hepatitis C (this risk is much less common than hepatitis B, but the risk is higher for those who have many sex partners, already have a sexually transmitted disease, or are infected with HIV).

Of people who get infected with hepatitis C, most develop a long-term (chronic) infection. Usually there are no symptoms. If the infection has been present for many years, the liver may be permanently scarred. This is called cirrhosis. In many cases, there may be no symptoms of the disease until cirrhosis has developed.

Hepatitis D virus (HDV) is only found in people who carry the hepatitis B virus. HDV may make a recent (acute) hepatitis B infection or an existing long-term (chronic) hepatitis B liver disease worse. It can even cause symptoms in people who carry hepatitis B virus but who never had symptoms. Some of its risk factors include:

❖ Abusing intravenous (IV) or injection

drugs.

❖ Being infected while pregnant (the mother can pass the virus to the baby).

❖ Carrying the hepatitis B virus.

❖ Men having sexual intercourse with other men.

◆ **HERPES SIMPLEX VIRUS (HSV-1 AND HSV-2).** This comes in two different categories, HSV-1 and HSV-2. HSV-1 is the main cause of herpes infections on the mouth and lips, including cold sores and fever blisters. It is transmitted through kissing or sharing drinking utensils. HSV-1 can also cause genital herpes, although HSV-2 is the main cause of genital herpes. HSV-2 is spread through sexual contact. You may be infected with HSV-1 or HSV-2 but not show any symptoms. Often symptoms are triggered by exposure to the sun, fever, menstruation, emotional stress, a weakened immune system, or an illness. There is no cure for herpes, and once you have it, it is likely to come back.

◆ **HUMAN IMMUNODEFICIENCY VIRUS (HIV).** The human immunodeficiency virus (HIV) is a type of virus called a retrovirus, which infects humans when it comes in contact with tissues such as those that line the vagina, anal area, mouth, or eyes, or through a break in the skin. HIV infection is generally a slowly progressive disease in which the virus is present throughout the body at all stages of the disease (there are 3 stages). HIV is in the blood and genital secretions of the infected person and it is spread when these secretions come in contact with tissues such as those lining the vagina, anal area, mouth, eyes (the mucus membranes), or with a break in the skin, such as from a cut or puncture by a needle. The most common ways in which HIV is spreading throughout the world include sexual contact, sharing needles, and by transmission from infected mothers to their newborns. Sexual transmission of HIV has been described from men to men, men to women, women to men, and women to women through vaginal, anal, and oral sex.

The best way to avoid sexual transmission is abstinence from sex until it is certain that both partners in a monogamous relationship are not HIV infected. Because the HIV antibody test can take months to turn positive after infection occurs, both partners would need to test negative for at least 12 and up to 24 weeks after their last potential exposure to HIV.

◆ **HUMAN PAPILLOMAVIRUS (HPV).** Genital human papillomavirus (also called HPV) is the most common sexually transmitted infection. There are more than 40 HPV types that can infect the genital areas of males and females; they can also infect the mouth and throat. Most people who become infected with HPV do not even know they have it. Most people with HPV do not develop symptoms or health problems from it. HPV infections can cause:

❖ Genital warts (usually appear as a small bump or group of bumps in the genital area).

❖ Cervical cancer (usually does not have symptoms until it is quite advanced) and other less common but serious cancers, including cancers of the vulva, vagina, penis, anus, and oropharynx (back of throat including base of tongue and tonsils).

◆ **HUMAN T-CELL LYMPHOTROPIC VIRUS (HTLV-1).** Human T-cell lymphotropic virus (HTLV) was the first human retrovirus discovered with its signs and symptoms as:

❖ Motor and sensory changes in the extremities.

❖ Spastic gait in combination with weakness of the lower limbs.

❖ Clonus.

❖ Bladder dysfunction and bladder cancer.

Transmission of HTLV-I is believed to occur from mother to child via breast feeding, by sexual contact, and through exposure to contaminated blood, either through blood transfusion or sharing of contaminated needles. The importance of the various routes of transmission is believed to vary geographically.

◆ **MOLLUSCUMCONTAGIOSUM** is a skin rash caused by a virus and it is transmitted by direct contact, either person to person or by shared items, such as clothing, towels, and wash cloths. It is likely that genital lesions are sexually transmitted. Lesions develop within two to three months after exposure. Some doctors consider MC a sexually transmitted disease in adolescents and adults and recommend that people with genital MC be tested for other STDs.

Abstinence between partners in courtship can help shield them from bitter emotions for one another, in the event that such courtship does not end in marriage.

Chapter

Four

The Conquering
TACTICS

Avoid hugging and kissing; they close
your minds to danger signals.

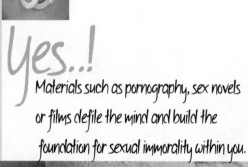

Yes..!

Materials such as pornography, sex novels
or films defile the mind and build the
foundation for sexual immorality within you.

Praying about the future with all diligence
has never stopped being the best way to lay
a strong foundation for your marriage.

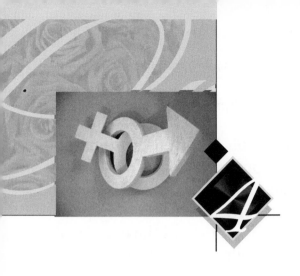

THE CONQUERING TACTICS

HANDS OFF. CLOTHES ON.

This is a position I sincerely must emphasize over and over again in order for you to get it straight. Some people prove that they don't involve themselves in sex but they do other things like kissing, pecking, smooching, etc. It may daze you to know that they all fall into the same category of sexual sins before God. When you 'hands off' it means no such things as smooching, and when you maintain the 'clothes on' position it means no sex. In order not to fall into the doom of pre-marital sex, hands off with clothes on. Avoid hugging and kissing; they close your minds to danger signals.

NEVER GET HORIZONTAL. REMAIN VERTICAL.

Getting horizontal is the lying posture for sex while vertical position is the pure friendship position for engaged partners. Though some people could remain vertical and still indulge in some ungodly acts, but you stand the chance of making yourself the enemy of God if you deceive yourself.

GET RID OF FILTHY MATERIALS, THEY DEFILE THE MIND.

Materials such as pornography, sex novels or films defile the mind and build the foundation for sexual immorality within you. And once those things get registered on your mind, it means you are in the trap already. It enlarges its coast in your thought flow and if you don't get rid of them, you will fall for it.

AVOID SPENDING TIME ALONE BEHIND CLOSED DOORS.

As long as you still wear the mortal body, temptation is an experience you cannot avoid. But in order not to fall victim, you have to avoid certain things. Staying behind closed doors and being alone with the person you are in love with can trigger the activities of the body chemistry. This is natural, hence you may not be able to pray against it. What you just need to do is avoid being alone where you might be tempted to fall for it and nobody will know anything has happened.

PRAY A LOT ABOUT THE FUTURE.

Whether you are presently engaged now or not, praying about the future with all diligence has never stopped being the best way to lay a strong foundation for your marriage. No matter how sure you are about things working out in your favour, pray, pray and keep praying! You can never pray enough when it comes to the issue of marriage, only the grace of God can actually cover up for us. So, pray without ceasing.

AVOID STEPS TO PHYSICAL INTIMACY SUCH AS:

i.   Looking at a guy/lady and making eye contact.

ii.   Holding hands. This is a nice sign of attachment. It says you like each other but it must not be done behind closed doors.

iii. Hands on shoulder and hands on waist. Though a definite sign that romance is in the air unfortunately it is only allowed for the married couple.

iv. Kissing on the cheek or softly kissing the lips. These are sweet, innocent signs of affection for married couples, not for the engaged partners, avoid it.

v. Petting while clothed.

vi. 'Experimental' nakedness.

vii. Sexual intercourse.

PRAYER POINTS

1. My God and my Father, let Your mercy connect my destiny to Your able hand, in the name of Jesus.

3. I break lose from the yoke of marital failure, in the name of Jesus.

4. Spirit of mistakes and error, my life is not your candidate, let me go, in the name of Jesus.

2. My Father, give me a miracle that will make me forget my past mistakes, in the name of Jesus.

2. Every power that hates to see me laugh, your time is up, die, in the name of Jesus.

3. Every power monitoring my marital life for

evil, scatter, in the name of Jesus.

4. My Father, change the rules for my sake, in the name of Jesus.

5. Any heavy yoke upon my destiny, catch fire, in the name of Jesus.

6. Every hand of man manipulating my life, catch fire, in the name of Jesus.

7. O God of Elijah, arise, disgrace my marital enemies, in the name of Jesus.

8. Blood of Jesus, correct my past, in the name of Jesus.

9. I fire back every arrow of the enemy, fired into my life, in the name of Jesus.

10. I remove my name from the register of darkness, in the name of Jesus.

11. In any way that my past is attacking my star, my Father, manifest your power and deliver me, in the name of Jesus.

BOOKS FOR SINGLES BY DR. D. K. OLUKOYA

1. Choosing Your Life Partner
2. Breaking The Yoke Of Marital Delay
3. 34 Laws Of Courtship
4. Dominion Prayers For Singles
5. Principle Of Magnetising Your Divine Spouse
6. 40 Marriages That Must Not Hold
7. Dating Plus

OTHER BOOKS BY DR. D. K. OLUKOYA

1. 20 Marching Orders To Fulfill Your Destiny
2. 30 Things The Anointing Can Do For You
3. 30 Poverty Destroying Keys
4. 30 Prophetic Arrows From Heaven
5. A-Z of Complete Deliverance
6. Abraham's Children in Bondage
7. Basic Prayer Patterns
8. Be Prepared
9. Bewitchment must die
10. Biblical Principles of Dream Interpretation
11. Biblical Principles of Long Life
12. Born Great, But Tied Down
13. Breaking Bad Habits
14. Breakthrough Prayers For Business Professionals
15. Bringing Down The Power of God
16. Brokenness
17. Can God Trust You?
18. Can God?
19. Command The Morning
20. Connecting to The God of Breakthroughs
21. Consecration Commitment & Loyalty
22. Contending For The Kingdom

23. Criminals In The House Of God
24. Dancers At The Gate of Death
25. Dealing With The Evil Powers Of Your Father's House
26. Dealing With Tropical Demons
27. Dealing With Local Satanic Technology
28. Dealing With Witchcraft Barbers
29. Dealing With Unprofitable Roots
30. Dealing With Hidden Curses
31. Dealing With Destiny Vultures
32. Dealing With Satanic Exchange
33. Dealing With Destiny Thieves
34. Deliverance Of The Head
35. Deliverance of The Tongue
36. Deliverance: God's Medicine Bottle
37. Deliverance from Evil Load
38. Deliverance From Spirit Husband And Spirit Wife
39. Deliverance From The Limiting Powers
40. Deliverance From Evil Foundation
41. Deliverance of The Brain
42. Deliverance Of The Conscience
43. Deliverance By Fire
44. Destiny Clinic
45. Destroying Satanic Masks
46. Disgracing Soul Hunters
47. Divine Yellow Card
48. Divine Prescription For Your Total Immunity
49. Divine Military Training
50. Dominion Prosperity
51. Drawers Of Power From The Heavenlies
52. Evil Appetite
53. Evil Umbrella
54. Facing Both Ways

87. Overpowering Witchcraft
88. Passing Through The Valley of The Shadow of Death
89. Paralysing The Riders And The Horse
90. Personal Spiritual Check-Up
91. Possessing The Tongue of Fire
92. Power To Recover Your Birthright
93. Power Against Captivity
94. Power Against Coffin Spirits
95. Power Against Unclean Spirits
96. Power Against The Mystery of Wickedness
97. Power Against Destiny Quenchers
98. Power Against Dream Criminals
99. Power Against Local Wickedness
100. Power Against Marine Spirits
101. Power Against Spiritual Terrorists
102. Power To Recover Your Lost Glory
103. Power To Disgrace The Oppressors
104. Power Must Change Hands
105. Power Must Change Hands (Prayer Points from 1995-2010)
106. Power To Shut Satanic Doors
107. Power Against The Mystery of Wickedness
108. Power of Brokenness
109. Pray Your Way To Breakthroughs
110. Prayer To Make You Fulfill Your Divine Destiny
111. Prayer Strategies For Spinsters And Bachelors
112. Prayer Warfare Against 70 Mad Spirits
113. Prayer Is The Battle
114. Prayer To Kill Enchantment
115. Prayer Rain
116. Prayers To Destroy Diseases And Infirmities
117. Prayers For Open Heavens
118. Prayers To Move From Minimum To Maximum

119. Praying Against Foundational Poverty
120. Praying Against The Spirit Of The Valley
121. Praying In The Storm
122. Praying To Dismantle Witchcraft
123. Praying To Destroy Satanic Roadblocks
124. Principles of Conclusive Prayers
125. Principles Of Prayer
126. Raiding The House of The Strongman
127. Release From Destructive Covenants
128. Revoking Evil Decrees
129. Safeguarding Your Home
130. Satanic Diversion of the Black Race
131. Secrets of Spiritual Growth & Maturity
132. Self-Made Problems (Bilingual book in French)
133. Seventy Rules of Spiritual Warfare
134. Seventy Sermons To Preach To Your Destiny
135. Silencing The Birds Of Darkness
136. Slave Masters
137. Slaves Who Love Their Chains
138. Smite The Enemy And He Will Flee
139. Speaking Destruction Unto The Dark Rivers
140. Spiritual Education
141. Spiritual Growth And Maturity
142. Spiritual Warfare And The Home
143. Stop Them Before They Stop You
144. Strategic Praying
145. Strategy Of Warfare Praying
146. Students In The School Of Fear
147. Symptoms Of Witchcraft Attack
148. Taking The Battle To The Enemy's Gate
149. The Amazing Power of Faith
150. The God of Daniel (Bilingual book in French)

ANNUAL 70 DAYS PRAYER AND FASTING PUBLICATIONS

12. Prayers That Bring Uncommon Favour And Breakthroughs
13. Prayers That Bring Unprecedented Greatness & Unmatchable Increase
14. Prayers That Bring Awesome Testimonies And Turn Around Breakthroughs